COMMANDO
CRAPS &
BLACKJACK

JOHN GOLLEHON
COMMANDO CRAPS & BLACKJACK

CARDOZA PUBLISHING
Las Vegas, Nevada

NEW REVISED EDITION!
Copyright © 1983, 1984, 2001, 2004, 2012 by John Gollehon
-All Rights Reserved-

Library of Congress Catalog Card No: 2011933351
ISBN 13: 978-1-5804-2299-4
ISBN 10:   1-5804-2299-3

Hurry up and visit our website or write for a full list
of Cardoza Publishing books and advanced strategies.

CARDOZA PUBLISHING

P.O. Box 98115, Las Vegas, NV 89193
Phone (800)577-WINS
email: cardozabooks@aol.com
www.cardozabooks.com

About the Author

John Gollehon is considered more than just an expert player; he is a trusted authority, having written extensively on all the games included in this book. Gollehon is recognized by the national media as an expert on casino gambling and is frequently cited in newspaper stories on gaming. He has also appeared on numerous television documentaries. Gollehon's writings span five decades, having first published a gaming newsletter in 1979. He is the author of 28 titles on beating the casino, many of them best-sellers.

In his books, Gollehon shows players the skills they need to build confidence and become a top player, teaching them the secrets of developing timing—when to lay back, and when to deliver that knock-out punch.

Cardoza Books by John Gollehon

Conquering Casino Craps
Commando Craps & Blackjack!
Casino Games
What Casinos Don't Want You to Know
Attack the Casino's Vulnerable Games

To Red Dog

When you play,
play with caution,
play with patience.
You can't win
without them.
—*John Gollehon*

From the Author...

Your decision to gamble is a personal one. It should take into account many things, not the least of which is your ability to wisely manage money. If you frequently overdraw your checking account, exceed your credit-card limits, or otherwise spend your money recklessly—buying on impulse, for example—suffice to say gambling is a bad idea.

If you do decide to try your luck, promise yourself that you will stay within your means. Playing craps can be fun. Don't let serious losses take your fun away.

A Note to the Reader

John Gollehon's extensive writings on casino gaming have now spilled into four decades, beginning with his 1979 newsletter. *Commando Craps & Blackjack!* is an exhaustive rewrite of his first book, *Pay The Line,* a book that became an instant classic in the early '80s and stayed in print for a remarkable eighteen years.

In this groundbreaking edition, Gollehon has added powerful concepts and strategies to what he credits as his most effective weapon—mastered over 30 years—in beating the casino at craps and blackjack. It's called *blitzing.* As you'll quickly learn, it's not a matter of simply striking, but striking *at the right time.* Over the years, Gollehon has refined and perfected these two potent components of winning—blitzing and timing—to chalk up his incredible win record.

Now he shares his hard won strategies with you.

TABLE OF CONTENTS

4. THE 10 RULES OF DISCIPLINE FOR GAMBLERS   41

5. CRAPS: HOW TO WIN!   61

1 INTRODUCTION

You can learn how to win if you sincerely want to. If you set your mind to it. If you can find the desire to stand up, challenge the casino, and break away from the passive crowd of losers.

Give *Commando Craps & Blackjack* a few hours of your time. On your next visit to a casino, you'll have a dramatically different attitude about gambling. You'll learn how to seek out only the most favorable playing conditions. You'll never again play in marathon sessions; instead, you'll learn the value of timed strikes with scheduled breaks in between. You'll never again begin play with large wagers; you'll work your way up if you're winning and you'll walk away if you're losing. You'll be doing things you've never done before, instantly recognizing the wrong moves you would have made previously. You'll have new confidence based on skill, control, and proper conditioning. You can play proudly, knowing you're going to be darn tough to beat! And isn't that what it's really all about?

Commando Craps & Blackjack isn't hype. It's clout—and plenty of it! Start at the very beginning and read every word. Reread any sections you don't fully understand.

Invest an evening in preparing yourself to win!

2 HOW TO BEAT TODAY'S GAMES

Craps and blackjack are indeed the casino's two most vulnerable games. They are also two of the most venerable. In one form or another, they've around for decades on end, evolving into a current hodgepodge of rules that vary from one casino market to another. In spite of this lack of a standard, one of the games—craps—has given players more benefits overall, regardless of the venue, as these past decades have marched on. Sadly, however, the other vulnerable game—blackjack— has lost some of its earlier benefits, particularly in the newer venues. Blackjack is still worth our concerted effort to defeat, and it can be defeated, but we have to approach it differently from the way we have approached the game in the past.

> Few players today fully realize that they need a new arsenal of weapons to beat blackjack and craps.

It's important that you know both games' track records of change so that you can appreciate the pluses and understand the negatives. It's always nice to know exactly where you stand, and I'm going to tell you in no uncertain terms. We can't play the games the way they were played in the '60s and '70s! We have to take them on with *today's* rules. Of course, we can't all play in Las Vegas, where game rules are arguably the best. There are an enormous number of casinos scattered over America, and I'm sure that at least one or two of them are close to you. We have to look at these new venues and the game rules that have been arbitrarily chosen. We have to learn how to beat the games against these new rules, and against different rules that vary from one venue to another.

Don't fret—it can be done. And we are going to do it!

NEW WEAPONS FOR WINNING

CRAPS

The biggest game improvement has happened at the craps tables, namely in a bet called an "odds bet" that you'll learn about later. The changes that have been made for this important bet are so significant that you might want to give all your attention to the dice tables. But maybe not. In spite of the fact that casinos everywhere have toughened blackjack, it is still a smart choice when you look at both games in terms of their sheer percentages, particularly over the long term. Although the percentage differences are not very much, blackjack still gets the nod, if only by a matter of one or two tenths of a percent.

BLACKJACK

When I first began playing casino games in the late '60s, blackjack was the only game I played. Single deck games were everywhere in Nevada, and the rules were so player-friendly that I always expected to win. And most often, I did. Well, you know what happens to all good things. As the 1970s rolled by, blackjack was reeling from casino countermeasures that had nearly ruined the game. But just as old plants die off and new shoots flower in the spring, so did a wave of new players who poked up their heads, mostly unaware of the changes in climate yet fully aware of blackjack's sizzling reputation. Reputations die hard. Even today many new players expect a blackjack game from seasons long past, a game that really doesn't exist anymore. And when they think they've found it, they try to beat this game of masquerade using old, worn-out ideas. It just doesn't work.

In the days when blackjack was so very, very vulnerable, it's fair to say that casino bosses quickly got tired of seeing their money scoot out the door. I remember a casino boss telling me that he considered the game to be a loss leader, to borrow a retail term. The game was ripe for picking and casinos simply let the money tree get picked and picked and picked. They hoped that some players would come in and play other games, or that unskilled players would sit themselves down and "subsidize" the winners. It didn't work and we can't go back. Those delicious days are gone.

Today we are faced with so many eight-deck games that *card counting*, a term you'll become very familiar with later, is no longer a viable option in its original concept. Later on, I detail three important things for you to do when you play blackjack, not the least of which is to count the cards, but in a new way. Eight decks will no longer hamper a good blackjack player; in fact, multiple-deck games may actually help us along as we use our new, modern weapons.

NEW PLAYING HABITS

In recent years, the playing habits of players for both craps and blackjack have changed. Blackjack has flattened out, no doubt for all the reasons I've cited. On the other hand, craps is enjoying a new birth. That change in the odds bet I alluded to earlier has clearly played a big part in its recent spurt of interest. Casino bosses had it all wrong years ago when these changes to craps and blackjack were made. They feared the new odds bet because they thought it would hurt their bottom line. But what did it do? It created a horde of new players, players the casinos want. The casino's reaction to card counting at the blackjack tables was an overreaction. The changes were too severe, which cut back on the number of players. And that's not what casinos want!

But what's done is done. Equipment manufacturers are building craps tables in record numbers, while blackjack players are taking it on the chin. It's time to weigh what we've learned and prepare to strike. It's time that *we* throw the punches! But to do that, we'll need to learn new playing habits. Of course, if you're a new player learning from scratch, you have no old habits to worry about. Your timing couldn't be better!

COMPARING OTHER GAMES

We can't move forward to the basics of craps and blackjack until we talk about all the new casino games that have popped up to rival the old standbys. I'll make this very brief. Here's what you need to know: Ignore them—forget them! All of the new poker-based table games are negative-expectation games, and that means exactly what you think it does. Forget low percentages. Forget positive expectation. Forget the idea of a fair bet. It ain't gonna happen!

Most of the new casino games are only a little better than roulette, and that's not saying much. Although I used to enjoy playing the wheel, in all fairness, I can't include it as a game worth this special effort. It's a game of timing: Either you time your choices right or you go down with the best of them. Roulette is so solidly entrenched in mathematical certainty that any hope for long-term success is pure foolishness.

Baccarat could easily be a game worthy of our special attention, but there are two drawbacks that must exclude it. For one, there are no strategies that can work because baccarat is purely a game of timing no different from roulette. For another, the high table-minimum bets go against the grain of the disciplines we will want to practice.

HOW TO OVERCOME LOSING

Before we learn the games, I want to make sure you can be a sensible, disciplined gambler Let me give you what a film director would call a "walk through." We're going to walk through a casino and see what players are doing; mostly, what they are doing wrong.

The chief reason for player failure in a casino hit me soundly over three decades ago as I watched a popular Nevada casino fill up with players. In a word: Apathy. Plain, unadulterated apathy. This particular casino offered the worst playing conditions imaginable, yet there was no shortage of players. I counted over 20 blackjack tables, all with six decks at a time when single-deck games could be readily found. Player options were severely restricted. Even the dice tables were all single odds, at a time when casinos were beginning to experiment with double odds as a means of attracting new players.

That evening, the casino was jammed. Players were drawn to this plush casino, obviously not aware that better games with far better rules were just across the street, an easy walk across the Strip in those days (today, you take a cab). I watched players splitting face cards and being afraid to hit stiffs. Indecisive! Like going to war without a battle plan. Players at the dice tables were making asinine bets one after another. People were lured into the keno lounge, making bets that rival the high percentages of today's state-run lotteries.

Most of the noise, however, was coming from the slot machines—and it wasn't the sound of money pouring out, but of money pouring in. No clattering of coins as they hit the tray, but that of coins being swallowed up: ca-chunk, ca-chunk, ca-chunk. It was a sound typical of that era, in contrast to today's credit-play slot machines that chew up your money with their mouths closed. The idea of adding electronic sounds to the machines hadn't been invented yet. Didn't anyone realize the odds of hitting five 7's? That's right, five 7's! The most popular machines of that time were five reelers where it was just darn tough to line up anything, let alone 7's. Not only were these players bucking odds of 3,200,000 to 1, they were playing for jackpots that paid only a fraction of the amount they pay today!

Just so you don't get the idea that things are better today for slot players, let me tell you what else has gotten bigger: the casinos' profits! Today, nearly 60 percent of gaming revenue comes from slot machines. And we can thank the '70s generation for ushering in the modern age of slot machines. Over the years, slot machines have become much smarter. Slot players, unfortunately, have not.

It dawned on me that the great majority of players in that particular casino had no concept of the games, no understanding of odds and percentages. No awareness of the variations in game rules that can seriously hamper their ability to win. Why didn't they know? Didn't anyone care? I honestly believe that even today, the casinos could take all the aces out of the decks and still pack the tables on Saturday night! I truly believe that. They could cram ten decks into the shoe and few players would care or even realize it. Then as now, Atlantic City casinos use eight decks for all but their "high roller" blackjack tables. Eight decks! Not exactly a treat for card counters because, at the time, an eight-deck shoe was considered virtually unbeatable. It's still not a treat today, but newer strategies have been devised to make eight decks a bit more palatable.

PREPARING YOURSELF TO WIN!

Let me ask you the same questions today that I asked 20 years ago. Do you know the correct player actions at blackjack—hit, stand, split, or double down—for all dealer upcards and player hand combinations? There is a correct action for each combination: It's called **basic strategy**. Did you know that? And do you know the answers to the following questions?

Do you know the variations in double-down rules? The different rules for splitting?

Have you ever tried counting the cards?

Are you aware of a super-powerful count system, the Imperial II Count Strategy, that's far and away the easiest to learn and play?

Do you know the difference between double odds and three-times odds, or even five-times odds? Do you even know what an odds bet is? No, it's not a blackjack bet, it's a craps bet, and it's the best bet in the casino! (If you don't know about it yet, you soon will.)

Do you know how to discipline yourself to play the right games, find the right tables, make the right bets, and quit with winnings in your pocket?

Do you know how to strike with a plan? To blitz the tables with a powerful assault. To grab the casino's money and run! Have you ever done this, or are you the type of player who likes to settle into a comfy table game and get pummeled?

Do you care, or do you just want to make your donation for another tortuous weekend of second-guessing yourself?

P.T. Barnum put it best with the overly used adage, "There's a sucker born every minute." It's just that most of them seem to hang around casinos. These players aren't gambling—they're giving their money away! They might as well write out a check, mail it to the casino, and save themselves some aggravation.

But no, for some reason, the great majority of players seem to take delight in losing.

STARTING OUT SMART

Repeat after me: We are *not* going to start out with big bets in craps and blackjack! Too risky. Not prudent. Especially when you consider all the new strategies we'll have to use. Why take added risk?

3 THE WINNING FORMULA

Winning at anything is an exciting experience that gives you a feeling of success that goes far beyond monetary gain. But in the casino setting, it's the monetary gain that casino "mercenaries" care about. It's all they care about—and that's the reason, believe it or not, why they don't win as often as they should. Hear me out.

Everyone wants to win. No one wants the stigma of being a loser. But just exactly how much do you have to win to be a winner? I guess the question pretty much identifies the problem. Certainly you can appreciate that there are values other than the dollar-sign value associated with winning, which helps to explain why some people can be thrilled with a $20 win, an amount that's little more than a gratuity for others. I can recall the days when winning $50 on a football game was totally satisfying. It might as well have been $500; the "win" made my weekend.

Fifty dollars wasn't going to change my lifestyle—the sheer pleasure was picking the winner! I felt as much a winner as the winning team I had bet on. It's important that you understand the psychology of this example because your attitudes and emotions play a critical role in winning, whether you win $50 or several thousand. Believe it or not, some players have not learned how to enjoy winning. They can only demand it: the more the better. And where would you suppose that attitude can only lead them? Over the years, I've taught myself to be happy with a win of any amount. Why? Because it answers my first and second rules of gambling: protect against losses, and take what you can get.

THE FIRST AND SECOND RULES OF GAMBLING

Protect against losses
Take what you can get

It may be elementary, but you must appreciate the fact that winning any amount of money is much better than losing any amount of money. If the winning sessions are small, let them accumulate. Or simply recognize that the playing conditions have toughened, and you'd better take the token win and be thankful. Sure, we all would like to win big, but we must learn to take wins, any wins, in stride. Train yourself to be happy with any win simply because it *is* a win. You're on the plus side of the ledger. Losses, especially those that follow winning sessions (giving your winnings back), can take a greater toll on your feelings, mood, and confidence level than the financial setback to your wallet.

CHANGING THE WAY YOU THINK

Every weekend, hundreds of thousands of players make their pilgrimage to their favorite gambling mecca, whether Las Vegas, Atlantic City, Reno, Biloxi, Detroit or a little Indian casino up the highway for "a little gambling." Ask anyone. That's always the answer: "We're going to do a little gambling."

It's not the same as heading out on a fishing trip to do "a little fishing," no sir. You head out on a fishing trip to catch fish. Honestly now, I'm sure you've never heard anyone say to you as they leave for Casino City: "We're going out to win some money." Nope! Gamblers don't expect to bring back much of anything, save the shirt on their back. The pretense of most gambling trips is based on negative conditioning, don't you agree? Not sure? Then let me help you with this one. I'll quote the complete version of the answer to why these weekend gamblers are heading to the tables: "We're going to do a little gambling, but we're not going to lose more than two or three hundred dollars."

> The typical gambler spends more time worrying about losing than forming an all-out attack to win!

Typical gamblers spend more time thinking about and worrying about losing, or at least limiting their losses, than forming an all-out attack to win! Do they have a burning desire to win? Apparently not. They have already conditioned themselves to lose. On that typical weekend, Interstate 15 is jammed from Los Angeles to Las Vegas, San Francisco migrates across Interstate 80 to Reno, and New York jams the Garden State Parkway to Atlantic City. The casinos have turned on their magnets, welcoming players with open arms, not to mention double odds and double decks. Believe this statistic: Over 95 percent of all players are not skilled, have no serious plan to win, and honestly anticipate losing. Not surprisingly, they go home losers.

It must be that most weekend gamblers simply like to play. Winning would be nice, but the real motivation is the fun and excitement of big-time gambling on that typical get-away weekend. They like the shows, the shopping, the pools, the gourmet dining, and the lavish, relaxing atmosphere of a big casino. Yeah, it's relaxing, all right—like a shot of Demerol just before your operation, an operation to remove your wallet!

POSITIVE THINKING

You can have an operation, too, but of a different sort. Let's call it "Operation Win." You're not going to the casinos to play, you're going there to win! That's your mission. And don't tell me that playing is fun. The two components of playing are winning and losing. Winning is fun. Losing is *not* fun.

Several years ago, I got caught in a radio interviewer's trap when we had a similar on-air discussion about playing for fun or playing to win. He pressed me about whether or not I enjoy playing; that is, just playing. "What about when you're only breaking even, not really winning or losing, and it goes on and on like that," he asked. "Is that fun?"

Frankly, I'm glad I was asked the question because it gave me a chance to do some self-analysis. My answer silenced him. I told him that when I'm playing and not really moving up or down, which we all know happens frequently, I enjoy the anticipation of winning. I enjoy knowing that there's still that big fish in the lake that nobody's caught yet. We all want to catch the big fish, but we need to know that someone else hasn't caught it first. It's no different in the casino: If we have a chance to win big and we do, we can always enjoy the anticipation of landing that big win! So what are we talking about here?

We're talking about positive thinking!

DO CASINOS ALWAYS WIN?

I get this question all the time. Apparently, all gamblers think that casinos always win. Let me give you the answer: Over the long term, they always win, absolutely. But over the weekend, they might not. And that's another integral part of your operation—Learn how to hit the casinos in the short term. Fewer strikes. More targets hit. You can't beat them every weekend, so let's stop those regular visits. What you need to do is stage surprise attacks—but you can't surprise them if they always know you're coming!

Let me put it this way: If the dealers all know you by your first name, you're making the trek too often. If you flat out refuse to cut back on all those frequent trips, then at least cut back on your actual playing time by making quick and frequent exits when you're not winning. That's right: If you're missing the target right and left, it's time to holster your weapon.

The number one fault of most gamblers is so appreciated by the casinos that they actually have coined a term for it. It's called "extended play." And that leads to the number two fault of most gamblers, exhaustion. Many gamblers play, and keep playing until they have exhausted their money or their time. They simply don't know how to quit. These playing habits I've just described help to explain how major-market casino resorts can capture nearly a million dollars a day in winnings. Half a million dollars a day is considered the industry standard.

Yes, casinos win. They win consistently over the long term, and poorly disciplined players simply make it easier for them. So does that mean that skilled, well-disciplined players can make it tougher for them?

Of course!

But no one's going to break the casino's bank. Occasionally, you'll hear about a big hotel-casino in financial trouble, but don't for a moment think that someone hurt the place at the tables. No matter how large the win, the casino will always bounce back. Even a red hot dice table won't show red ink on a casino's financial statement. If a casino is losing money, it's usually the result of mismanagement, questionable investments, or start-up costs.

DO YOU GAMBLE FOR ENTERTAINMENT?

In today's casinos, it's easy to do—just one more example of how we fall into a casino marketing department's trap. We're not there to gamble, we're there to play games. A casino is a giant playground for grown-ups. That's the way casinos want us to think. To help create this facade, slot machines have been redesigned to look like arcade games, certainly not money-grabbing, in-your-face slot machines. And most players play along with this ruse—they play the machines as they would play a real pinball machine to win free games. If they win a few dollars, they think of it in terms of winning more minutes to play! Concerts, lounge acts, greeters, and even jugglers and clowns add to the circus atmosphere. The casino is simply just a part of the show.

And speaking of concerts, you should know that many hotel casinos in smaller-market venues increase their room rates when a special concert is scheduled. That's right: If you show up on Thursday night expecting a lower weekday room rate and find out that Hootie & the Blowfish is appearing in the showroom, expect to pay the top room rate. Even if you don't give a hoot about Hootie, you're subsidizing the show anyhow through the higher room rate—through the nose.

But forget the showroom for a moment. Let's get back to the casino. Spare me the silly excuse of counting your losses—and you will have losses if you think this way—as the cost of entertainment. If you're going to a casino with your hard-earned money just to be entertained at the tables, let me make a suggestion. Let me make several: There's golf, the movies, shopping, dining, golf, sightseeing, hiking, boating, and did I mention golf? That's right, there are so many other forms of legitimate entertainment to consider. Heed my two important rules: First, never ever consider gambling as a form of entertainment. By doing so, you're simply providing an excuse for losing. Second, never ever try to teach your spouse how to play golf.

Let's get serious for a moment. It's easy to see how so many players can write off gambling as a cost of entertainment. Clearly it is their lack of preparation—I'm talking about mental preparation. Going in, you need to know that you can win this fight, and it is a fight. You're fighting for the casino's money, and the casino is fighting for yours.

TAKING CONTROL OF YOUR GAME

Go get yourself a CD of Rocky's theme song and play it every time you pull into a casino's parking lot. Throw a towel around your neck and punch the air as you jog your way to the front door. Well, tone that down a little, but you get the idea, right? I want to see you psyched up for that knockout punch, fully cognizant of everything that's going on, with all of your senses on full alert. Can you do that?

An old friend of mine has a ritual he goes through the minute he arrives at a casino, before he goes looking for a craps table. He finds a remote spot away from the congestion of people. Standing off to the side, he closes his eyes and takes deep breaths. He tunes out all the sounds, and changes the visuals on his mental screen. The picture he brings up is of piles of chips accumulating in front of him as he throws winning number after number. When he feels that his confidence to win is overflowing, he opens his eyes and heads straight to the tables like a robot. If there's an open spot, and if he's going to be the next shooter, he takes his position. Otherwise, he keeps walking and waiting—waiting for the right time, because he must be the shooter. He must be in control.

It's been years since I've played beside him, but I can tell you that he plays with a level of conviction that I rarely see anymore. Craps is no fun and games, it's serious business for him. And you know what? The other players at the table quickly sense his confident nature, and they pick up on it too. All of a sudden, the dice table has changed. That's the effect he has on people. Trust me, he's the kind of guy who can change a room the moment he walks in. He can also change a dice table—and the dice will oblige.

Comparing my friend of years ago to today's typical player is no comparison at all. Even the more active gamblers fall short. Though they are better players armed with a strategy, a plan, and a serious approach, they all blend in among the masses. They are "casino-oriented," as the bosses like to call them, which I'm not sure is a compliment or not. Chances are, the players' skills are limited to their basic knowledge of craps, the payoff odds, the probabilities of the numbers, the varying rules, and hopefully, some basic discipline about money management. If the players are blackjack stewards instead, they probably know basic strategy well enough to keep the game on a fairly even keel. Hopefully, they know enough about card counting to at least keep a side count of aces.

But this overview of the better players has some serious holes in it. Nine times out of ten, what's missing is the discipline to follow tough rules, personal rules. The casinos all have their rules, which they follow to the letter. You also need your own set of rules, plus the discipline to make them work for you. Even that isn't enough. You need to unleash your intuitive senses, just as my friend used to do. You need to take control. It always amazes me how most players ignore any perceptions that might signal a change of course. Open your eyes! Is there something you don't like? Is there a bad vibe coming from a certain player, a certain dealer, a certain table? We're not robots going through the motions. We are human beings with a wealth of experience behind us. Use your intuition. Call it up and let it come to the forefront. Let it guide you to the success you seek. Let it be your friend.

TRAINING YOUR BRAIN TO WIN

The next time you plan a trip to your favorite casino, consider a new definition for winning and losing. Winning is being successful; losing is being a failure.

Does this sound different? "Failing" sure sounds a lot worse than "losing," doesn't it? No one wants to fail in business, in marriage, or in school. Those are scars no one wants. But for some reason, failing in a casino is an accepted failure. Most players have trained themselves to accept a gambling loss, I guess, because most everyone else does. Do you enroll in college with that same apathetic outlook? Would you consider getting married with that same complacent attitude? I would hope not. Then why is a gambling failure any different?

> If you win, you succeed. If you lose, you fail.

Even for the small bettor, when you add up the losses over several years, you might be looking at several thousand, maybe tens of thousands of dollars. This is no time for apathy. Gambling is serious business. Treat it that way! I'm not suggesting that you beat on yourself every time you lose. I'm simply saying that you can get accustomed to losing if you take such a careless attitude about it.

Here's the flip side of all this. The answer to preventing yourself from becoming conditioned to losing is to become success-driven, a trait that manifests itself in an intense dislike for failure. To be perfectly blunt about it, I hate losing. I never accept it as routine, not in the casino or anywhere else. Nor should you. Successful people think of winning as a fight against failure. I don't accept winning as routine, either. It's just like the topic we talked about at the top of this chapter: being content with small wins. Any win prevents a loss, remember? Psychologists believe that there is a hidden motive behind success-driven people: They do not want to cope with failure.

Start using these new definitions: If you win even a few dollars, you are successful; if you lose even a few dollars, you fail. See if this exercise in semantics puts a new spin on your gambling attitude. It should.

You will work harder to win—to be successful—because you don't want to fail.

DEALING WITH LOSING

I'm sure there aren't too many other gambling books on the shelves at Barnes & Noble that have a subheading like this one. Pretty negative, huh? No, it's not negative at all. In fact, finding the correct way to deal with losing sessions represents a positive. A very important positive!

And although we just learned that success-driven people hate it, as I hate it and hopefully you hate it, there are always times when losing stares us right in the kisser. That's right. I know this won't come as a big surprise to you, but losses are inevitable. Some players can handle a loss from both the financial aspect and the emotional impact. Some can't. Don't think that all players are not affected inside by a particular loss: It happens to almost everyone.

In my own case, however, I would never let a loss reach the proportions where I would suffer either financially or emotionally. But I wouldn't be entirely truthful if I said there isn't any aspect of gambling that can actually bother me, and I think you know what I mean. I mean in a nagging sort of way; nagging at me for several days after I return from a gambling trip.

What is that one aspect of gambling that really bothers me? It's playing poorly, making stupid mistakes. Yeah, I do it too, and I should know better. Sometimes my poor play gnaws at me more so than a losing session. Case in point: I once played at a craps table in a Northern Michigan casino and couldn't believe the shoot a young lady was having. I was snake-bit from an earlier session that didn't fare so well, and it showed in the way I was betting this lady's incredible hand; namely, very, very conservatively. Any idiot could see that this was not the time to be conservative. If there's any particular part of my play that I pride myself in, it's knowing how to take advantage of those rare hot streaks. If anything, I'm usually too aggressive. But not this time: I played like a down-and-outer down to his last few dollars. All the way home I recited the "if onlys" and the "shouldas" and "couldas" until I drove my wife nuts. "I should have ten grand in my pocket. No, make that *twenty* grand!" Okay, so much for the therapy session. Let's get on with the issue at hand.

Guarding against damaging losses is really a matter of setting limits. In my own case, I follow a strategy I devised decades ago that prevents me from going over the edge. In fact, it keeps me at a good, safe distance from the edge. But when you get right down to it, it shouldn't take a strategy to stop you—plain common sense should step in, but that doesn't always work either. We'll talk about dealing with big losses later. Right now, the issue is losses that fall within your limits. How do you respond to those losses?

If you're typically a bad loser, gambling is a bad idea. I'm not talking about how you hate losing—I'm talking about how you react to it. You know how you react to losing a tennis match, an important account, or a big contract. How do you deal with it? Do you act like an adult or a child? If you throw your club because you hit your ball into the woods, first consider growing up, and then consider gambling (and maybe a golf lesson wouldn't hurt either).

I told a story during the taping for a television documentary on gambling that had the producers in stitches. It was about a blackjack player who would hit the padded surround of the table every time he lost a bet. The larger the wager, the harder he hit the table. Well, he finally ran out of chips so he ordered another marker for $5,000. When the chips were delivered to him, everyone gasped as he pushed the entire stack into the betting circle. The gods of chance were really fed up with this guy, so they made him squirm a little as the bet played out. He was dealt a 12 against the dealer's 10. He took a hit and got a deuce for a total of 14. Wow, the pressure! Another hit and another deuce, for a total of 16. Beads of sweat are running down his forehead as he motions for another card. He draws a four and makes a total of 20. He can relax. Or can he?

The dealer turns over a 3 with her 10 for a total of 13. Things are looking up. She draws a 3 for a total of 16 as the player rubs his hands in eager anticipation of a beautiful bust! She draws 5 (you knew it was coming, right?) for a total of 21 to beat this poor loser in the most painful way. Actually, there's more pain coming. Before she could pull away his chips, he slams his hand on the table so hard that he broke the plywood top. The next morning, a pit boss told me the rest of the story. They had to take this jerk to the hospital because the table wasn't the only thing he broke. He had fractured his hand in five places. The hand surgeon was baffled when he tried to repair the broken bones. Turns out that the player's hand had been broken many times before—in exactly the same places!

Putting the worst-case examples aside for a moment, we all know that a gambling loss, especially at the top end of a player's limits, can cause certain players much more than a short-term reaction. The frustrations may drift over into their everyday life at home and at work, putting a damper on just about everything and taking the polish off their otherwise enjoyable activities. If this is a problem you can relate to or you suspect it could happen to you, the solution is not necessarily to stop gambling. Indeed, losses occur everywhere every day, not just in casinos. Sure, I personally suggest that you do stop gambling, but how do you stop the other losses that bring on the same consequences? I'm not a psychiatrist, but I strongly believe that the best way to counter the damaging effects of a loss is with a win! Find things, or make things happen, that represent a win to you.

Earlier, I referred to losing as a failure and to winning as a success. Perhaps the real reason that losses (failures) nag at some people is a distinct absence of successes. If I lost all the time, I'd probably be in a bad mood, too! In baseball, when you score a run, it's a success; when the other team scores a run, it's a failure. At the end of nine innings, the team with the most runs is usually in the best mood.

Score some runs!

I realize this book is about winning, and here I am talking about losing. But without this vital preparation—knowing how to deal with a loss—you are not a complete player. You are not a survivalist. You can't carry out your mission to defeat the casino until you know how to defeat adversity.

THE ADDICTIVE GAMBLER

On a recent golf outing, I played in a foursome with three of my best business customers that, quite frankly, I wanted to impress. I can usually break a 90, but on that particular day I played very poorly. I missed easy putts, drove the ball out of bounds at least twice, and even shanked a tee shot! Embarrassed? It was more than that: I felt like a complete loser! I'm sure my playing partners were wondering if I was as incompetent in business as I was on the golf course. When you're on the golf course, your business successes and other personal accomplishments take a back seat to your golf game. Strange, isn't it? At that moment, your game is all that counts. I forgot about the successful aspects of my life, all the positive things that keep me going. All I could think about was shooting one of the worst rounds of my life at the most inopportune time.

The disgust of playing like a weekend duffer grew bigger with every hole. Finally, on the 18th green, I had a chance to salvage the day with an easy par putt, no more than three feet from the hole. At least I could have ended the round on a positive note. When I walked up to the putt, I didn't study it for some reason as I would usually do. I didn't take any practice strokes, either. I just hit it. The ball ran at least ten feet past the cup. I then completed the four-putt for a fat triple-bogey 7!

I putted the ball as though I didn't want to make it, as if I purposely wanted to miss my par. Why? Could it have been that I wanted to punish myself for playing such a lousy round? You bet it was! I missed that putt because I felt that I didn't deserve it. And here's the kicker. Leading psychiatrists believe that compulsive gamblers continue to gamble for exactly the same reason. They *want* to lose! It's hard to believe, but they actually want to punish themselves for all the previous losses they've stacked up—and for not having the discipline to change or stop.

Make sense? How could anyone purposely want to lose? It made sense in my golf story, why not in gambling? Yes, self-inflicted punishment is one of the main reasons for compulsive gambling. An urge to self-destruct. Low self-esteem. These are the things that really drive the compulsive gambler. It's an ugly addiction that I hope you never have to worry about.

In case you still can't believe it, here's another example that might be closer to home. Most people today are very concerned about their appearance. It seems that everyone exercises and jogs to keep fit and in shape, but what about people who are overweight? To some people, being thin is an obsession. They can't stand being fat! Ever notice what happens sometimes if a friend calls attention to a person's weight problem with an unsolicited, none-of-your-business comment like, "Why don't you go on a diet?" The sheer mention of their weight problem will provoke them and bring on more eating, as if they're doing it to spite their friends. In fact, they're spiting themselves! Knowing that more eating will put on more weight is punishment for being overweight in the first place.

There's yet another reason for compulsive gambling that is equally hard to believe. It deals with the individuals who are so straight, so perfect in every detail, that it appears they have no failures! Perhaps they are successful athletes, stars in sports, who don't drink, don't do drugs, and don't even smoke. Perfect specimens. Know the type? Well, gambling can put an end to their misery—yes, misery! People are not allowed to be perfect; everyone is supposed to have a vice. "There must be something wrong with me if I'm perfect," isn't that what most people would think? Gambling becomes an outlet for failure. It makes up for an otherwise impeccable life. They feel better. Doesn't make a bit of sense, does it? It's hard to figure, but the reasons I've just cited are medical fact, tricks of the mind.

Hopefully, one good way to put an end to this gambling compulsion is to simply identify it—and that's what I've done for you in the following paragraphs. We'll start with a self-inventory of questions for you to answer.

5 KEY QUESTIONS

Before you wager a single dollar, ask yourself five important questions—and answer them!

1. WHY DO I WANT TO GAMBLE?

If you're not sure why you want to gamble, don't even consider it. Your indecisiveness may be trying to tell you something. You must respond immediately to that question. Your answer must indicate a strong desire to win! Never gamble just for the fun of it. Never go gambling on a whim.

2. CAN I AFFORD TO GAMBLE?

If there's reason to believe that you can't really afford it, don't do it. There are no guarantees. If money's tight and the house payment's due, why risk it? Gambling should be on the very bottom of your list of things to do with your money.

3. DO I HAVE A STRONG DESIRE TO WIN?

If you're not positively sure you seriously want to win, you probably won't. It's that simple. When the time comes to strike, you won't have the toughness to win. Part of winning is your attitude, which affects your preparation, commitment, discipline and desire. It has to be there, all of it.

4. CAN I BE SATISFIED WITH A SMALL WIN?

Do you know what it means to quit winners? It's a term in gambling jargon that means quitting when you're ahead of the game. What it doesn't mean is winning and then giving it all back because you wanted to keep playing. If you're an average player with an average income, will a couple hundred dollars make you happy? Is that enough?

5. HOW MUCH IS ENOUGH?

I've asked this question before, but I must ask it again before we move on. If you're only interested in a big score, I urge you to stay out of casinos. You are a perfect example of the casino's preferred player: You're a victim of greed, the casino's biggest ally.

Don't get me wrong. There's nothing wrong with setting your sights high. I hope you win thousands and thousands of dollars! But heed this: In the casino, you must have the ability to recognize an opportunity, the wisdom to know that you can't force it to happen, and the discipline to quit when it's gone. In the real world, you can make your own opportunities. In the casino, you can only look for them. If you managed to win $200 during a brief opportunity, why give it back as you fight for the big score when the opportunity has long vanished? My advice: Stuff the $200 in your pocket. Maybe you'll appreciate it more when you're away from the tables.

In the next chapter, we'll go into some ways to maintain your discipline while you're gambling, including some extremely important rules you must follow to become a consistent winner.

> In the casino, you must have the ability to recognize an opportunity, the wisdom to know that you can't force it to happen, and the discipline to quit when it's gone.

4 THE 10 RULES OF DISCIPLINE FOR GAMBLERS

At first glance, this chapter may seem out of place. Logically, we would now begin to discuss the games in general and learn how to play—and win—with new and exciting strategies for you to enjoy. Not yet!

This chapter may very well be the most important of the entire book. Each sub-heading is a Rule of Discipline that you positively must respect, believe in, and abide by without fail. You've made it this far, but we have got one more step to go. That's right, this chapter is the third and final installment of basic training.

As you read the key points in this chapter, ask yourself, "Can I do this? Do I believe it? Do I understand why?" If not, proceed no further! There is little reason to learn new strategies to raid the casinos' coffers if you're going to shoot blanks. I'll teach you where to aim, give you the ammunition, but you are the player who ultimately has to pull the trigger.

1. GREED IS A LOSER'S ALLY

We've already discussed what winning must mean to you. Remember, winning must be reduced in your mind to its simplest terms—if you have won any amount, you have not lost! You must be content with a win of any amount. Why? I just told you why. Because it helps ensure our first objective: not to lose.

Reverse psychology applies here. I'm not just teaching you how to win, I'm teaching you how not to lose. Let small winning sessions accumulate. You'll be pleasantly surprised when you count the bills in your back pocket. That's right. The bills that you didn't think amounted to much.

If you thumb your nose at small wins and small opening wagers, pushing harder and harder with your bets to find that big win that never comes, think hard about where it's taking you. Look back on your experiences and ask yourself if this is the way you want to continue fighting. Aren't you battered enough? It's the first Rule of Discipline: Greed is a loser's ally. In other words, greed makes losers out of winners.

2. KEEP YOUR PLAY IN THE SHORT TERM

There are honest-to-gosh professional gamblers who live in Nevada, play regularly, and win regularly. Unlike the Hollywood image you might conjure up of real, professional gamblers, you'll be surprised to learn that their initial bets are rather modest. If they don't plunge their way in, right out of the chute, why should you?

You shouldn't. This isn't a race, there's no clock to beat. Sometimes, winning takes more time than you might imagine. But the pros have all day, and all night. It's a long day at the office and a tough way to make a living, but few complain.

Playing for long hours seems to conflict with my earlier advice of limiting your time at the tables. But there's a big difference here. Craps is a negative-expectation game. Blackjack is mostly negative expectation, but not always. And these are the games that most of us play. They are not, however, the "games" that the pros play. They bet sports, they bet the ponies, they bet poker (the real game, not the machine version). These games are not negative expectation in the strict sense. Assuming a top level of skill from these players, they have a different respect for time than we do. The longer they play, the more likely they will win.

I don't consider myself a professional player, not in the sense that I gamble to put food on the table. I doubt very much that you are either, nor should you want to be. There are far easier ways to make a living. If you have a choice, you should become a brain surgeon. So what do we do if we want to win at negative-expectation games? We play in the short term. We look for short-term anomalies where we can cash in. We look for streaks, we look for fleeting opportunities.

That's right: We're looking for a quick strike!

It's the second Rule of Discipline: Keep your play in the short term. Play short sessions and take frequent breaks. Learn how to hit and run! Marathon sessions will not win the war.

3. SET LIMITS ON YOUR LOSSES BUT NEVER ON YOUR WINS

A casino executive once told me that the house makes more money on progressive slot machines (a bank of connected machines with an ever-growing jackpot) than on regular machines. The reason, though, is not the obvious one. It's not just because these machines get more play, which they do. It's because slot players give it their all—all their money! There's no quitting. Not until the money's gone. It's an all-or-nothing approach to gambling that simply doesn't work. If you've tried it, you know it.

Video poker players are the most notorious example. Many players go for the royal flush and only the royal flush. It's their only goal; they will exhaust their stake to get it. The smaller hits along the way will just add bullets to their arsenal. But they will fire every round if they have to. And they usually do. But do they score the royal? They usually don't.

I don't like using slot machines as examples in this book, but in this case, it's a perfect one. Slot players, for the most part, rarely leave a machine with a goodly portion of their investment. Table players usually leave with something. It might not be much, but it might be enough to start the next session.

We talked earlier about quitting winners. Quitting when you're ahead. It's tough to do. But you know what? It's tougher to quit when you're losing. That's called *quitting losers*. And to be able to do it without reservation is the mark of a top-rank player.

Think of it this way: You know you're going to have to quit a session sometime. You can't play forever. Wouldn't it make more sense to quit when you're ahead? But what if you're never ahead? Then you have to quit losers; you have to take that bitter pill without wincing. The question, I guess, is just exactly how many of those bitter pills do you want to take? The longer you wallow through a losing session, the more pills pile up in front of you.

It's the third Rule of Discipline: Set limits on your losses; but never on your winnings. So where do you set those loss limits? Set them lower than you would like. And stick to them. Make sure your bankroll can carry you through all your planned sessions. Quitting is easier when you realize that much of what makes gambling fun is the anticipation of winning.

Remember? There's always another session to look forward to.

4. NEVER TRY TO FORCE WINS BY BETTING RECKLESSLY

I'm sure you've noticed players who walk up to a blackjack table and ask for a marker for thousands in chips. The first bet is so predictable. Probably $500, maybe more. You know the minimum color is black, so forget a stack of green chips as you or I might bet if we're riding a nice streak. But these guys don't think the same way we do. They figure they can create their own streaks. They believe they've timed it perfectly so they start shooting before they even know what they're shooting at! They have no patience to start at a safer betting level and then hopefully work their way up.

What they're doing is what I call trying to force wins by the way they bet. It's probably the dumbest move in the casino. The cards don't know how much anyone's betting. And I doubt if they care. The big guns aren't going to pull out a streak. A nice streak happens when it feels like it.

By starting out conservatively, you'll have a better chance of being there when it happen—if it happens. It's called "staying power." You need staying power to stalk the streaks. I've always said that these big shooters walk up to a table to impress themselves with their fireworks display, but they forget that fireworks end with the grand finale. Fireworks start slow and build.

When I see a player kick off a session with a "grand finale" wager, I assume he has money coming out of his ears and his brains are right behind. It's insane to begin play with large bets. It defeats every plausible rule of commonsense wagering. Casinos love players like this. And that should tell you something.

It's the fourth Rule of Discipline: Never try to force wins by betting recklessly.

5. NEVER LOSE SIGHT OF THE VALUE OF MONEY

The big shooters I alluded to in the previous piece would laugh at the amount of my beginning wagers, usually about $15. I'm popping three reds in the circle while these morons are loading up with monster chips.

If you would ask the big bettors why they begin so strongly with these large wagers, their answers are quite predictable. It's usually either of two responses:

1. "My lifestyle is different than yours. My $500 equates to your $15. I make more money than you do. What can I say?" Well, I know what I can say, but I want to keep this book clean.
2. "I gamble for excitement. I need that big bet out there to feel the tingle. I want a jolt when I win." But don't they feel the jolt when they lose? Sure they do. And they want that, too.

Okay. Let's find the flaws in their reasoning. It's easy.

First of all, if the wide variation in bet size is merely an equalizer in earnings and lifestyle, that's suggesting that there are multiple values of the same money. But there aren't. A dollar is a dollar. A hundred dollars is a hundred dollars, whether it's in their pockets or ours. A hundred dollars buys the same stuff for them as it does for us. Do they pay more for a Big Mac at McDonalds than we do? When you start losing sight of the singular value of money, you start losing sight of values in general. Eventually there may be no values left at all.

That's right, having a lot of money is a poor excuse for betting a lot of money. And I can assure you that these players who put tons of money on the line didn't earn it through years of hard work. If they did, they would have more respect for it. No. The money must have come easy. It certainly goes easy.

Now about that other reason. Gamblers who want to feel a little jolt should just stick their finger into a lamp socket. It's cheaper. The gambler who needs to feel the tingle should take up bungee-jumping or something. Oh, what some people give for a little excitement.

Sure. A casino is a good place to find excitement. It's also a good place to make excitement. And therein lies the problem. You should know that gamblers who want to create excitement themselves by taking huge risks are at the forefront of addiction.

The fifth Rule of Discipline is indeed a serious one: Never lose sight of the value of money. And never risk it for excitement. You should know that all big bets don't come from rich players, and all rich players don't make big bets. Players who pretend to be rich by the way they bet are usually the problem gamblers. Not surprising, is it? Would you be surprised to know that most rich players have enough sense to keep it in check? Well, it's true.

Let me tell you about a guy I ran into many years ago at a craps table in Las Vegas. Here's a gentleman having the time of his life making five-dollar bets. If he wanted to, he could buy the casino. Probably would pay cash for it! I told him to work his bets up a little. He was winning, so it was sensible advice. But he appeared nervous and unsettled with the "big" bet out—all of twenty-five dollars! He wanted only to win and to enjoy the time. A loss might have upset him. A big win would have meant nothing to him. He makes thousands of dollars a week just managing his investments!

Before we go on to the next rule of discipline, allow me to amplify on what we've just learned. I'll need to take you back many years to the days when I first began playing craps. Yes, they actually had dice tables back then. Don't get smart with me.

I played with a friend from California who was in the music business, as I was at the time, and we would always meet in Vegas after our yearly trade show in Anaheim in January. But as the years went by, we added a summer trip together, and then a fall trip, and, well, you get the idea. We liked playing together. We liked winning together. And for some reason, that happened an uncanny number of times.

I learned early on not to get crazy at the tables. I played with the same starting wagers and followed the same betting strategies throughout our many escapades to Fun City. In other words, I didn't try to win more by betting more. I simply hoped to win. More would have been nicer, but winning was the goal for me. I always enjoyed the anticipation of large wins, but I never got carried away with it. Not so for my friend. He gradually built up his betting levels—something I didn't notice at first, but after a few years it became obvious. He was betting out of control.

The thought of playing at my level, the same as his level when we first started, was not even remotely feasible. He was now making more money; he was now bored with his job. I remember his saying as we stood against a dice table, "My life isn't as exciting as it once was. I get my excitement right here." Well, he wasn't the same friend I remembered. He made me nervous as I watched him toss hundred-dollar chips on the table. No. Not bets—tokes for the dealers! His betting was simply out of control and I couldn't stand to watch him play anymore. He would walk away from a table with a look on his face that I remember to this day. His look was a cry for help.

It was ten years later when I ran into him at the music show. I was out of the business by then but I wanted to go out there and see old friends. He looked thirty years older. He had lost his job and found a new one, several new ones. His wife had left him, and he was basically alone. The dice tables broke him.

I remember from the days when his bets started climbing, his asking me why I always play with red chips, asking how I could possibly have any fun with those. I told him that I start out with these table-minimum chips because I love the game too much. But he didn't understand what I had meant.

Too bad! I was telling him that I never wanted to reach the point, as he later would, where I had to stop because I couldn't trust myself to play sensibly anymore. If you love the games as much as I do, respect them not for what you can win, but for what you can lose.

6. BET SAFELY AND KEEP YOUR WINNINGS!

Believe it or not, if you or I were to make a $500 bet, it could very well be called a safe bet. It just depends on when you're making it. The conservative betting I've been talking about is only for the start of a session, or when a session is not panning out exactly as you had planned.

I have nothing against a $500 bet. In fact, I often make bets that are much more. And I hope you do, too, when the time is opportune. But never begin play with such a large bet. I know. I've said it before. But it's that important. You haven't tested the waters, and you might be risking a substantial portion of your bankroll.

Testing the waters? Is that what I just said? Let's find one of those types who likes to walk up and take the plunge at the table-games, and then let's pose a simple question. Here's one of those jokers walking by...

"Hey, buddy! Got a question for you: If you were going to go swimming in a quarry, or a lake or pond for the first time, what would be the first thing you would do when you got there?

"Right, but I mean *after* you take off your clothes.

"Yeah, right, but what would you do *after* you've had a couple beers?

"Check it out? Thank you. That's the answer I was looking for. What? No, not for girls, for rocks, you moron! Are you going to jump in without first checking to make sure there are no rocks barely submerged that you might crack your head on? You would? I'm relieved. Can you remember to always do that?"

And to my readers: Can you remember that, too? What's the point of jumping into a blackjack game or a craps game, without first checking for rocks?

Personally, I probably hold the world's record for table watching in casinos. If there's a rock, I'll find it. You'll never see me open my wallet at a table that shows no excitement and few chips in front of the players. And I better see dealer busts at the blackjack tables and pass-line wins at the dice tables, or I will not play. It is obviously no assurance that those favorable conditions I'm looking for will continue, but I would rather put my money on a continuation than on change. Will a cold table change for me the moment I walk up? Based on all my years of playing, I'll choose to go with a table that has already warmed up.

So let's say that you have checked out the tables, you've found a good candidate, you've begun your play by making safe bets, and now you've accumulated some nice wins. It's time to find the guts to start moving up in your wagers. Increase your bets by 30 to 60 percent as long as you continue to win. Enjoy your ride up. But when the ride ends, it's time to become conservative again as you look for another streak to ride.

Can you see the important difference in when to make the big bets? There's little risk betting a large sum when you're up four or five times the amount of your wager. You're betting back a portion of your winnings against the house. Casinos bosses consider this type of betting action as dangerous—for them! What you're doing is giving them a good shot at your small bets, then beating them over the head with your big ones. Relentlessly, you play them tough. A smart bettor!

There are times more frequent than you might imagine when you are well ahead during a typical playing session. Set aside some of those winnings by putting the chips in your back pocket, give them to your spouse or a friend, or hide them in your shorts. I don't care how or where you do it, but do it! The idea is to get them off the table and out of your sight. It's analogous to putting money in the bank. The practice will assure that you quit winners!

Play the few chips you have left after you've deposited your "save" chips, and try to build them up to a new plateau. Quit if you lose them. Casinos hate players who put chips in their pockets. By doing so, you've ruined their shut-out. You've already chalked one up in the win column. You continue to play without pressure. You know you've beaten them!

If my save chips happen to be black among a rack full of red, green, and black chips, I have to tell you that sometimes I hope a boss is watching me as I reach for my black beauties, hold them firmly in my hands as I count them and caress them and gently slide them into my pocket. (You can probably tell I've always wanted to write a romance novel.) The boss and I will make eye contact, and I'll communicate a silent message: You can't have these! They're mine now! You won't get them back!

The sixth Rule of Discipline involves a series of smart moves. Look for the right table, start with safe, conservative bets, build your bets up if you catch a nice streak, and always stash away a goodly portion of your winnings to take home. And remember that if you don't catch a nice run of wins early, quit the session. You can always try again later, hopefully under better circumstances.

7. TEMPER YOUR ANXIETY

A friend of mine who goes to Las Vegas regularly always comes back a loser. He hurries to the hotel, hurries to find a valet to park his rental, hurries to check in, and then literally stumbles over his luggage to get to the nearest craps table. Forget the room. The room can wait. This guy has some serious losing to do. No time to wind down from the long flight, no time to relax. This is a story that really doesn't have to be finished. You can write your own ending.

My friend, incidentally, is not greedy. Don't confuse greed with anxiety. My buddy is simply so anxious to play, that he, well, plays, and plays. I recall the last time we played together. The bellman took his luggage to his room. My friend took his wallet to the craps table. Long story short: He never saw the inside of his room. In fact, he never saw the inside of a restaurant. I'm not even sure if he saw the inside of the men's room! Boy, was this guy wired!

I always make it a point before I leave home to schedule something to do for when I arrive at a casino—something other than gambling. Let's be honest. Many of us tend to have a high level of anxiety when we arrive that needs to be tempered. It's human nature. In fact, some psychologists, including the noted gambling expert, Marvin Karlins, says in *The Book Casino Managers Fear The Most,* that a reasonable level of anxiety is probably good for you.

But just to make sure that I'm not so wound up as to make stupid, costly mistakes at the tables, I do insert a buffer between my arrival and my gambling. It might be something as simple as a business meeting, or as relaxing as a nice dinner in one of the casino's gourmet restaurants.

Visitors to Las Vegas are rarely conditioned for play as well as the locals who live there. Gamblers who live in Vegas are already there! There's no long flight. No long drive. They can be in a casino within minutes! With spirits flowing! Obviously, locals must follow their own strict rules on gambling or they can't live there. It's that simple. You can't live there and gamble like the conventioneers do. I'm sure you can appreciate that. The locals, many of whom I know well, are perhaps the most disciplined of all gamblers I've known. They have to be.

The seventh Rule of Discipline: Temper your anxiety. Never play if you are unable to focus on your objective. If you are tense or restless or those spirits are really flowing, avoid the temptation to play. You must "reschedule."

Don't let your enthusiasm get in the way of your common sense.

8. AVOID COMPS LIKE THE PLAGUE

I'll make this one short and sweet. Like barkers on the midway, casinos offer you free room, free meals, free points, free cash, free anything—but comps are not free! Comps are the casinos' most effective marketing tools. Comps get you in, comps keep you playing.

The casinos love players who love comps. That should tell you something. Comped players tend to bet more than they want to, and play more than they want to, just to earn comps. Comped players give generously to the casino because they have lost their Number One objective. Too bad they don't give their losses to the Cancer Society, an orphan's fund, an animal rights group, or just send it home to their parents, or save it for their kids education. Oh, you don't think you're a philanthropist? If you're a comp player, your contributions to the casino's own fund is enormous! Comps pull out more profits for the casinos than any of the other traps they set for you.

A friend of mine says that if you're playing for comps, you're playing "under the influence." I couldn't say it any better.

I'll always remember the lecture I got from a player who just couldn't get enough of the comp scene. He showed me just exactly how serious he takes this thing by pulling out at least 50 slot-club cards from his wallet. We're not talking Visa Platinum here. These are just cards that any hayseed can get by filling out a form full of personal information. The cards serve a dual purpose: The casino can keep track of your bets, and they can lure you back through offers in the mail since they have your address.

The casino wants you! No, actually, the casino wants your money! You are just an insignificant carbon life form.

As he was showing me his comp-cards and telling me about all the neat things he plays for, I told him, "I don't want any casino keeping track of my bets!"

"But John, look at this. See this card?"

"Yeah."

"Right now this card will get me two hot dogs at the casino across the street! Free! And I'm not talkin' just any hot dog, these dogs are a foot long! Let's go eat one."

"Yeah, but I don't want to go to the casino across the street. The casino across the street is a dump."

"Yeah, but the hot dogs are free!"

"Tell ya what. You go. You can eat mine. And I'll see you when you get back."

He came back a little dejected.

"What's the matter?" I asked. "Weren't the hot dogs any good?"

"Oh, yeah, they were okay, but I got snagged by this uncooperative video poker machine over there."

"That's because they have the worst video poker machines in town. I don't even trust them. I don't even trust the casino! Don't you see it now? The free hot dogs were just to get you in there. It's like a carnival side-show where guys try to lure you into a tent where you can see, for a price, some guy with a penis growing out of his head."

"Really?"

"What do you think? It's just rubber and they glue it on? Now listen, throw the stupid cards away, okay? Start playing to win! And I don't mean stuff. I mean money. Don't be so gullible, okay?"

"Okay."

The eighth Rule of Discipline: Avoid comps like the plague, okay? It's like I told a pit boss at a small Indian casino where I play frequently. He stopped me as I'm leaving a table with a big handful of chips and said, "I've seen you here before. I don't think we have you on file."

"Right, you don't."

"But you can't earn any comps if we don't know who you are."

"That's fine. I won't trade my anonymity for a little ticket that says I can go stand in a VIP line for your $19.95 buffet."

"But you don't understand. You don't have to pay $19.95. It's *free!*"

"No, you don't understand. I want to pay for it. You know why? Because I never want to be tempted to play for it! I only play to win."

9. NEVER BUCK A TREND

Let's say you've read in the sports section that the White Sox are on a 12-game tear. They've also won 15 of their last 16 games. You've studied the pitchers and you've looked at the line. Now what do you do? You either bet the Sox or you pick another game! If you've won ten hands in a row at blackjack, continue with your progression upward. Don't pull back. I've heard insane reasons for jumping out of a streak, but none make any sense at all.

There's yet another example of bucking trends, and it comes from an incident that I'll never forget. As you know, I like to size up tables before I sit down to play, and on this particular day, a table was hard to pick. Most of the tables looked bleak. Actually it was the players who looked bleak. Tables don't change their expressions—or do they?

Anyhow, I noticed a table that had just emptied. And I mean *emptied.* Everyone left at once. Well, I've got to check this out, right? Did somebody throw up or what? The dealer was a very attractive lady who had no trouble attracting players. She just couldn't keep them. So, like an idiot, I sat down, fearing that I might be in for a shelling but also thinking that a good shuffle might change the cards.

Yeah, right! She looked at me with her big blues and said something to me that I'll never forget: "Do you really want to play at this table?" I kidded her about not having any customers. Casinos call players "customers," which sounds a little weird when you hear it. I mean, J.C. Penney has *customers,* casinos have *players.* Anyhow, I decide to become her customer, and, while she shuffles six decks of cards, I ask her if she's winning or losing, as if I didn't suspect. "I'm strong," she says. "No one's beaten me all day."

Well, I played through the shoe and watched her turn over 19's, 20's, and 21's to no end. She dealt me those great 15's and 16's that seemed to bust every time I took a hit. If this were not a first-class casino, I would have thought a ringer was dealing to me. But no: She was exactly as she had said she was. She was strong. As I limped away from the table, she reminded me what she had told me when I first sat down. Boy, talk about bucking a trend!

Today, instead of asking a dealer if he or she is strong, I simply watch a few hands to see for myself. Same goes at the dice tables. Is there a trend? If it's a bad trend, I have no business trying to break it.

Here's the ninth Rule of Discipline that you'll be tested on in the casino time and time again: Never buck a trend! If red has come up six times in a row at the roulette wheel, a wise gambler stays with red. Don't use the negative thinking that a positive run is about to end as your reason for not grabbing on—or worse, going the other way. Similarly, don't think that you can break a negative run by enforcing a superstition or some other irrational means. Trends, whether negative or positive, end or change without any contribution from players.

10. CASH IN ON WINNING STREAKS

After a big winning session, some players have a tendency to get a little cocky. They remember not only that session but the winning sessions before. It's called "selective memory," and the only time it's a good thing is when you're counting up your strokes on a golf hole. "Uh, I think I had a par." But in the casino, you conveniently forget the losing sessions, especially the big losing sessions, and begin thinking, "Hey, this is easy!" In short, you become arrogant.

Well, it's not easy, my friend. Sometimes, wins come so quickly that they overwhelm the inexperienced player. So what's next? Another session, maybe another casino, and the rookie player is expecting the same easy wins. Surprise!

When I was talking about trends a few paragraphs ago, what I didn't say and shouldn't need to say, is that trends are completely unpredictable. Otherwise, this would be easy! Dice are capricious. They go from sweet to sour in a flash, and only the rookies believe that it's a temporary setback. Cards at the blackjack tables turn faster than the Indianapolis 500.

If you think you can ride out a down trend, it might cost you your earlier winnings—but players do it all the time. It's the arrogance of players who think they can just walk up to a table and it will be no different from yesterday when they won so much, so quickly, so easily.

Some players actually take the "can't lose" approach following a huge win, but they are in for a big and sudden surprise. They will give the winnings back ten times faster than they won it. That fast! Casinos have studied this effect of negative and positive trends (they prefer the term *trend* rather than *streak*), and claim from the results of these studies that they win more when a table is cold than they lose when a table is hot.

The results of that survey speak volumes about the way players play. But casinos have a bonus going for them as to why most players do not take more out of a winning streak. Most players simply do not bet a winning streak heavily enough. They are either late getting in, or too timid along the way.

Incidentally, when I looked at these studies, I concluded that the terms of the negative trends lasted far longer, on average, than the terms of the positive trends. Although I found flaws in those studies, the basic idea that negative trends last longer than positive trends is inarguable. And you can credit the percentages for this imbalance in trends, not to mention the inept players whose continued presence keeps negative trends running.

It's good information to know, and it's our tenth Rule of Discipline: You must cash in on winning streaks for all that you can muster, because there is no equality between winning and losing.

> "Far better it is to dare mighty things, to win glorious triumphs, even though checkered with failure, than to take rank with those poor spirits who neither enjoy much nor suffer much, because they live in the grey twilight that knows not victory nor defeat."
> *Theodore Roosevelt*

I am closing this chapter with Roosevelt's famous words and one of my favorite quotes. It's a great motivational piece for those who are not risk-takers. But I must tell you that the gist of the quote is not that you go to a casino all fired up and then proceed to lose the farm. No, that's not the gist at all. To suggest relevance to casino players because casino players are risk-takers is absurd. Teddy's words are to encourage risk-taking *at* the right time. And I'm sure he wouldn't mind if I add "...with a little common sense sprinkled in."

In the casino, there is only one right time when it would make sense to throw a little more risk on the fire. That one time is when you are well ahead and riding a hot streak. That's the time to reinvest some of your winnings. I don't win big money by starting out with big bets. That's the wrong time! I make big money by betting a streak—but first I have to wait for it. So we should sprinkle a little patience in, too.

10 SHOTS OF WISDOM

1. Greed makes losers out of winners
2. Learn to hit and run
3. Discipline is a skill
4. Money management is the key to winning
5. Having a lot of money is a poor excuse for betting a lot of money
6. Respect the games not for what you can win, but for what you can lose
7. Setting aside some of your winnings is like putting money in the bank
8. Don't let your enthusiasm get in the way of your common sense
9. Never be tempted to play to win comps—play to win money
10. Don't try to break a bad trend

5 CRAPS: HOW TO WIN!

Craps fits the theme of this book—quick, commando-like strikes—better than any other casino game. And that's mostly because of the streaking nature of the game. Astute players look for a quick streak of winning numbers, grab their winnings, and make their escape. It's a perfect battle plan. But there's one problem. I guess you could call it "building up the ranks."

You see, most new casino players—and there are hordes of them—think of craps as the most complicated, difficult-to-learn game in the house. Why? Because the table layout looks complicated. There are so many different types of bets. So much confusion with chips flying everywhere. Sometimes 7 wins, sometimes it loses. There are stacks of chips scattered all over the layout. Most of these bets are in boxes in front of the dealers, but how does anyone know which bets are which?

Unfortunately, many gamblers shy away from craps because they assume it's too difficult to learn, let alone master. Hey, if you're going to fly this mission, you've got to sit in the cockpit and learn what all those gauges and instruments and levers mean. You're in luck. This is not an F-16, this is Wilbur and Orville stuff. Thinking that craps is complicated is probably the biggest misconception in the casino. Craps is plainly not complicated at all. It just looks that way!

THE ONE SKILL YOU NEED TO WIN

As any experienced dice player knows, craps is easy to play—and perhaps the easiest to learn too. More importantly, craps can be the most exciting game in the casino. But most important of all, craps offers the best wager in the house—a bet that doesn't give the house an advantage! And there are other "best" bets, too. In fact, among the non-skill table games, craps ranks first in terms of player potential. Among the skill table games, poker ranks first and blackjack is a distant second.

> Craps offers the best wager in the house.

With so many new players coming on board as new casinos open left and right, the non-skill games are the attraction. New players have shown a keen dislike for textbook-type study of a casino game. I can't blame them. The typical casino player has changed dramatically over recent years, and that probably explains why craps has grown rapidly in popularity. Craps is a low-percentage, non-skill game that can reap big rewards for the skilled bettor.

That's right. Learning how to play the game is easy. Knowing how to win at this game (making the right bets at the right time) requires a special discipline. Yes, discipline is a skill—make no mistake about it! Now you know why we spent so much time in the three preceding chapters learning betting disciplines. This is the game where you'll use your new betting skills more often than in other games.

Let me put it another way: This is the game where your new betting skills will have the best chance of paying off!

UNDERSTANDING THE DICE

To understand the game, let's first consider the dice. There are two dice in play, with each cube having six sides: 1 through 6. That means that numbers from 2 through 12 can be made when two dice are rolled.

Let's make an important distinction right now. The odds of rolling these 11 numbers vary. They are not all the same. The odds of rolling a 4, for example, are much higher (harder) than rolling a 7. There are only three ways you can roll a 4 (2-2, 1-3, and 3-1), but there are six ways you can roll a 7 (2-5, 5-2, 1-6, 6-1, 3-4, and 4-3). We'll get into all the probabilities in detail later on, but for now, it's important that you realize this fact from the outset.

THE PASS-LINE BET & COME-OUT ROLL

Let's list the numbers somewhat out of order so that you can best see what the numbers mean for the most common dice wager, the pass-line bet. Here are the numbers in groups for you to remember. Always think of the numbers exactly as I've separated them. It's important to remember the point numbers in the pairs as I've listed them. You'll find out why later in this chapter.

2-3-12	7-11	4-10	5-9	6-8
Craps (Loser)	Natural (Winner)	Point numbers (Must be repeated to win)		

Each of the numbers 2, 3, and 12 is called a **craps**, and it's a loser on the first roll, called the **come-out roll**, for all bets on the pass line.

Each of the numbers 7 and 11 is called a **natural**, and it's a winner on the **come-out roll**, the roll made before any point has been established. The remaining numbers 4, 5, 6, 8, 9, and 10 are called **point numbers**, and when one of these numbers is rolled on the come-out roll, that same number must be rolled again before a 7 is rolled in order to win the **pass-line bet**.

A new come-out roll always follows a pass-line decision, win or lose. If a 7 rolls on the come-out roll, the pass line wins. If a 3 rolls on the come-out roll, the pass line loses. If a 6 rolls on the come-out roll, there is no win-or-lose decision at that moment. The shooter rolls again, and again, however many times necessary, for either the 6 to **repeat** (in which case, the pass line wins), or for the 7 to roll (in which case the pass line loses). All other numbers are of no significance to the pass-line bet while the **shooter**, the player tossing the dice, is trying to repeat a point number (called "rolling for the point").

Now you can see why the 7 sometimes wins and sometimes loses. If the 7 is thrown on the come-out roll, it wins. But if the 7 is made while the shooter is rolling for the point, the 7 loses in what is called a **seven-out**.

The dice then pass to the next player, moving in a clockwise direction, and it becomes that player's turn to shoot, starting with a new come-out roll. As long as a shooter does not seven-out, the shooter retains the dice. Incidentally, if it's your turn to shoot, and you don't want to shoot, that's fine. Simply tell the dealer to "pass the dice," and then it becomes the next player's chance to shoot.

When you become more familiar with the game, I'm sure you'll want to shoot. It's fun! All you have to do is toss the dice to the opposite end of the table from where you're standing, and try to bounce both dice off the far wall of the table. It's easier to lightly toss the dice than it is to roll them, especially if you're standing at the far end of a table. There's no skill involved, in spite of the fact that many dice players have this notion that there are good shooters and not-so-good shooters. It's all a part of the game, just one of the many unique aspects of craps that makes it so exciting.

This is a typical Las Vegas layout, although some newer layouts follow the Atlantic City rule of eliminating the "Big 6 and 8" bets on the corners. It's a silly bet that pays 1 to 1 (even money) if a 6 (or 8) is rolled before a 7. The bet should pay 6 to 5. Even a place-bet on 6 or 8 will pay 7 to 6. Players who bet the Big 6 and 8 are showing their inexperience.

Another variation is the field-bet, where some layouts pay double on *both* the 2 and 12. Others pay triple on *either* the 2 or 12, as shown here (triple on 12). Most new casino venues are using the "Las Vegas" layout.

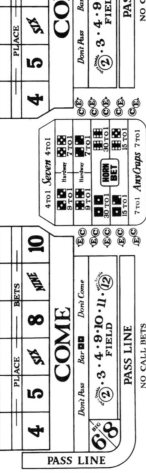

This layout is typical of Northern Nevada casinos. One of the major differences between the two layouts is the location of the "don't pass" and "don't come" sections. The Las Vegas layout has a section reserved for "don't come." Northern Nevada combines the two bets in one section. The other major difference is the odds expression for "prop bets" in the center of the layout. Notice that the Nevada layout defines the odds payout on a hard 8, for example, as 9 to 1. On the Las Vegas layout, the odds are defined are 10 *for* 1. Both expressions are the same. Odds of 10 for 1 just sound better and may lead unsuspecting players to believe they are getting a better payoff. It's a cheap ploy the casinos should be ashamed of.

FOLLOW THE PUCK

Now let's pretend to walk up to a table. Look at the illustration of the table layout. Notice that the area marked "pass line" runs completely around the player sections of the table in order that all players have a spot to make this wager directly in front of them. Also notice that both ends of the table are identical. The right side of the layout is only for players standing at that end of the table. If you're at the left end of the table, you need only concern yourself with that part of the layout.

When you first walk up to a dice table, how do you know if the shooter is about to make a come-out roll or if the shooter is rolling for the point? The **dealer** at the center of the table, who controls the movement of the dice with a hooked stick, will usually alert everyone at the table what's going on. If the shooter is about to make a come-out roll, the dealer will announce that the dice are "coming out." If the shooter is rolling for the point, the dealer will make that clear also by announcing, "The shooter's point is 8," or simply "Rolling for 8."

Another way to make this determination is to look at the numbered boxes at the back of the layout and locate the **puck**, which has a white side and a black side. The white side says "ON" and the black side says "OFF." The puck is about four inches in diameter and looks like a hockey puck, so you'll have no trouble finding it.

Those big boxes at the back of the layout represent the point numbers. At each end of the table there's a box for the 4, 5, 6, 8, 9, and 10. If the shooter is rolling for the point, the puck will be placed within the box of the point number the shooter is rolling for. When the puck is placed in one of these point boxes, the white side (ON) is up. If the puck is in the box marked "SIX," that's the point number the shooter is after.

If the puck is placed with the black side (OFF) showing, it's usually found in an adjacent box marked "Don't Come," which relates to an entirely different bet, but that's the spot the dealers use to place the puck when the next roll is a come-out roll.

As you might imagine, it's more likely that a shooter will be trying to repeat a point number when you walk up than to be throwing a string of craps or naturals on a come-out roll. So at that instant that you walk up to the table, the shooter will probably be rolling for the point. Possibly, you timed it perfectly and the shooter is about to make a come-out roll. That's your signal to make a pass-line wager. Incidentally, never make a pass-line bet while the shooter is trying to repeat a point number because then it's a bad bet. I'll tell you why later on.

When the shooter wins, everyone on the pass line wins! Unlike street craps, all the players at the dice table are playing against the house, not each other. In gambling jargon, the house is "banking" the bets.

LEARNING THE ODDS!

The next bet to learn is called an **odds bet**, and it's directly associated with the pass-line bet that you now know how to make. But before we can understand the odds bet, we have to learn what odds means, and what the correct odds are at a dice table for all the possible numbers. It's important that you know the odds because it tells you how you will be paid when you win. It's your way of checking the payoff to make sure you were paid correctly.

Probability Chart

NUMBER	WAYS	PROBABILITY	HOW
2	1	35 to 1	1-1
3	2	17 to 1	1-2, 2-1
4	3	11 to 1	2-2, 1-3, 3-1
5	4	8 to 1	1-4, 4-1, 2-3, 3-2
6	5	6.2 to 1	3-3, 2-4, 4-2, 1-5, 5-1
7	6	5 to 1	1-6, 6-1, 2-5, 5-2, 3-4, 4-3
8	5	6.2 to 1	4-4, 2-6, 6-2, 3-5, 5-3
9	4	8 to 1	3-6, 6-3, 4-5, 5-4
10	3	11 to 1	5-5, 4-6, 6-4
11	2	17 to 1	5-6, 6-5
12	1	35 to 1	6-6
	36		

Looking at the Probability Chart, it is readily apparent that there are more ways to roll a 7 than any other number. We know there are 36 ways to roll the dice. We also know there are six ways to roll a 7. That means there must be 30 ways to *not* roll a 7 (36 minus 6). So, our odds of rolling the 7 are 30 to 6. Dividing both numbers by 6 gives us odds of 5 to 1.

The Odds of Rolling a 7

Will Not Happen— **5 to 1** —Will Happen

└─+─┘ Total Number of Trials = 6

Out of six rolls, one roll should be a 7, and five rolls should be some other number. That's 5 to 1 odds. Notice that I said, "should be." The actual results may deviate somewhat over the short term, and that's what a smart dice player is looking for— an opportunity when the odds have wavered. But over the long term, a 7 will come up once in every six rolls. Never argue with the laws of probability!

WHO HAS THE ADVANTAGE?

Now that you understand odds at the dice table, let's go back to the pass-line rules and see how you stand. Let's see who has the advantage.

Okay, we know there are four ways to throw a craps and eight ways to make a 7 or 11. Wait a minute, we have an edge here! You bet we do. The player always has a strong advantage on the come-out roll. There must be a catch. And there is. The point numbers! When the shooter has established a point, the casino gets the edge, but not by much. Again, it's easy to see why. There are six ways to make the 7, and remember that the 7 loses when a shooter is rolling for the point. No point number can be made six ways. Your best chance of rolling a point number before a 7 is if the point is 6 or 8, since both of these numbers can be made five ways.

Never make a pass-line bet after the shooter has established a point number. That's a dumb move! You're giving up the best part of a pass-line wager—the come-out roll—where you have an edge, and you're getting down just at the time when the casino gets the nod. Not too smart!

The next logical question is, "Who has the edge when you take both the come-out roll and rolling for point numbers into account?" Not surprisingly, the casino gets the prize, but it's a cheap one. Overall, the casino advantage is 1.41 percent.

A PROBLEM FOR YOU TO SOLVE

The best way to fully grasp the probabilities of dice is to work out a problem on your own. Let me give you an easy problem to work on, all by yourself, and with the aid of our Probability Chart. What are the odds that a shooter will throw a point number on the come-out roll? Your answer will yield an important probability to always remember.

Now, find a piece of paper and a pencil, and work out the solution. But I'll only give you five minutes. That's all I'll wait, so get going.

Done? What did you get? You should have figured 1 to 2, or you flunk! Here's how we find it. We know there are 36 ways to roll the dice, right? And we know that all the ways to throw only a point number are 24.

POINT NUMBERS	WAYS EACH	TOTAL WAYS
6 & 8	5	10
5 & 9	4	8
4 & 10	3	6
		24

If we subtract the 24 ways to make a point number from the 36 total ways for all numbers, we have 12, which obviously is the total number of ways not to make a point number. So, odds of 12 to 24 are easily reduced to odds of 1 to 2. That's our answer! Incidentally, the 12 ways not to make a point number are obviously the six ways to make a 7, the two ways to make an 11, and the four ways to roll any craps.

Give yourself an "A" if you got it right. If you figured it out in your head because (a) you couldn't find a pencil, or (b) you didn't want to mess up this book, give yourself an "A+."

ODDS EXPRESSED AS A PERCENTAGE

When odds are expressed as 1 to 2, it means that in three trials to make an event happen, one time it won't happen and two times it will. If we want to express the odds as a percentage, as is often done, we simply divide the number of times the event will happen (the second number in an odds expression) by the total number of trials (both numbers in an odds expression). In this case, we divide 2 by 3. That's the fraction 2/3 (fractions are yet another way to express probabilities) and a percentage of 67 percent. There is a 67 percent chance that our shooter will indeed make a point number on the come-out roll.

1 to 2 Odds Expressed as a Fraction, Number, Percentage

$$\frac{\text{NUMBER OF TIMES AN EVENT WILL HAPPEN}}{\text{TOTAL NUMBER OF TRIALS}} = \frac{2}{3} = .666 = 66.6\%$$

When odds are expressed as a decimal number such as .67, it's interesting to note that these numbers are "maybe" probabilities in the short term. But there is a finite range to these probability numbers, beginning with 0 and ending with 1. If an event cannot possibly happen, the number is 0. If the event will positively happen, the number is 1. In between are all the shades of gray between black and white. You'll be happy to know that there are no other ways to express a probability that I know of. If there are any others, I don't want to know about them.

Even experienced gamblers are sometimes confused about odds, mainly because of the terms that are used to express them. If I were to say that the odds are "better than even," it means the same as "less than even." Such odds could be considered "low" or "short." The opposite terms would be "greater than even," "high," and "long."

In a horse race, let's say the favorite is going off as a huge 1 to 9 favorite (**short odds**), and the longest of the longshots is going off at 50 to 1 (**long odds**). It's easy to see the comparison if we convert these odds to decimals and then to percentages, as we did in our test question. If we divide 9 by 10 for the favorite, that horse has a 90 percent chance of winning, at least according to the oddsmakers who made the betting line. But our longshot does not look promising when we divide 1 by 51. That's only a two percent chance. Notice how one number is close to 0 and the other is close to 1. We've taken the extremes in this theoretical race, so we should expect the decimal numbers to approach the extremes also. Let me know when you divide out a horse's odds and come up with 1—I'll meet you at the track!

If you are learning about odds for the first time and trying to keep up, you might accuse me of writing a trick question because the numbers appear to be turned around. Always remember that the first number represents the likelihood of an event not happening. Based on the way I purposely phrased the question, the answer of 1 to 2 is correct. The first number is smaller than the second number because the odds are less than even (1 to 1) that the event will happen. If the odds of the event happening are greater than even, as is more often the case, then the odds are obviously expressed with the larger number first.

If the question had been phrased, "What are the odds that a shooter will *not* throw a point-number on the come-out roll?" the correct answer would have been 2 to 1, because the odds of the shooter not making a point number are greater than even. Another way to say it is "1 in 3."

Now you can see why we combined the point numbers in our earlier chart—6 and 8, 5 and 9, and 4 and 10. They were combined because the ways to make them are the same for both numbers in each pair. Accordingly, when odds are given for any point number, it's always the same for its sister point number in the pair.

> Remember the point numbers in pairs.

THE ODDS BET

Now that we really understand odds, we can learn how to make the important **odds bet.** This wager is made only when the shooter has established a point number. Place your odds bet directly behind the pass-line bet, but not in the pass-line area.

The casino will allow you to bet an amount that can be more than your pass-line bet. How much more depends on the casino. Some casinos will allow only two-times odds, called **double odds**. Some casinos will let you bet three-times odds, called **triple odds**. The more aggressive casinos may go as high as five-times and even ten-times odds. There are casinos in Las Vegas that often banner their craps odds on their marquee, boasting 100-times odds! What's the big deal, you ask?

The odds bet is a fair bet. The casino doesn't earn a penny on this wager. It's paid at the correct odds of rolling a point number before rolling a 7. Your wager on the pass-line is only paid at even money, regardless of the number. But the odds bet is paid at **true odds.** It's the bet that fortunes are made of!

Here's a chart that gives you the correct odds of repeating point numbers before a 7 rolls. It's important that you remember these odds because they tell you how you will be paid if you win.

POINT NUMBER	CORRECT ODDS OF REPEATING BEFORE A 7
6 & 8	6 to 5
5 & 9	3 to 2
4 & 10	2 to 1

Let's say that the shooter established 4 as the point. If you have $5 bet on the pass-line, you can make an odds bet of $15 at a triple-odds table. If the shooter successfully repeats the 4, you will be paid $5 for the pass-line wager and $30 for the odds bet! Look at the chart. The correct odds of repeating a 4 before rolling a 7 are 2 to 1. That's why your odds bet won $30.

The odds bet is just another example of why the game of craps is unique. There is no other bet in the casino that does not provide a casino advantage! Logically, you might ask, "Why make such a big deal about a bet that only evens out over a long term?" Let me answer your question with my own question: Would you rather make bets that always give the house a rock-solid advantage, or would you prefer a bet that's truly fair? A bet in the casino that doesn't favor the house is a big deal!

Making the odds bet along with the pass-line wager reduces the casino's total pass-line advantage from 1.41 percent to about 0.85 percent—and that's important. Double odds reduce the house edge even more to about 0.63 percent. Triple odds and ten-times odds and so on can reduce the percentage even more, to well under one-half percent! Although the odds bet does not directly affect the house percentage on the pass-line part of the wager, it does lower the percentage for the total amount of your wager. And in reality, that's what you should be concerned about.

The key to using multiple odds bets is in the way you size your bets. Let's compare a pass-line wager of $15 with no odds to another pass-line bet of $5 with $10 in odds. If the point is 10, you would be paid only $15 in winnings for the $15 pass-line wager, compared to $25 for the $5 pass-line bet with $10 in odds. See? It depends on how you structure your bets to earn the advantage of multiple odds without increasing your total risk.

It's worth noting, however, that high multiple odds can be risky. Even triple odds can sting if the dice are not **passing** (winning), so use common sense in making these bets. Some players use the odds bet as a betting progression of sorts, starting out with double odds and then moving up to triple odds, then four-times odds, and so on for as long as winnings accumulate. If they lose a bet, they go back down to double odds and start over.

It's a betting strategy well worth considering and one that I strongly recommend you use.

THE COME BET

The **come bet** is best described as a delayed pass-line wager. There's no question where to place it, since the largest block of the table layout is assigned for come bets. The area has the name "COME" boldly displayed in the center. You make come bets while a shooter is rolling for a point. That's the only time you can make a come bet, since it's basically just like a pass-line bet. And the same rules apply, which I'm sure you have memorized by now: With a 7 or an 11 wins on the come, and a 2, 3, or 12 loses. Any other number becomes the point number and must be repeated before a 7 rolls in order to win.

Let's say the shooter's point number to win on the pass line has been established as 6. If you wish to have another bet working for you that's just like the pass-line bet, simply place your bet in that section of the come area nearest to your position at the table. Hope for either an 11 or a point number, because a craps will lose your come bet, while a 7 will win your come bet but will lose the pass line. Let's say the next number rolled is a 9. Now you'll be looking for another 9 (before a 7) to win your come bet. It can be said that you have two numbers working: 6 **on the line** and 9 **coming**.

When a 7 or 11 is rolled while your bet is sitting in the come, the dealer immediately places the payoff directly beside your bet. It's your responsibility to immediately pick up the chips; otherwise the bet works on the next roll as another come bet. On the other hand, if a craps is thrown, the dealer simply takes your come bet and it's up to you if you want to make another bet. If the roll is a 7, the winning come bet is called a **last come**, and is often forgotten by players making it, especially if that 7 signaled a time to quit. Dealers often yell to players as they exit the table, "Hey, buddy, you forgot your last come!"

THE POINT BOXES

Come bets are settled in the come for rolls of 7 or 11 or craps, but if the roll is a point number, your come bet does not remain in the come area. The dealer will reposition your bet in the proper **point box** for the point number rolled, and in a spot within that box that's directly referenced to your location at the table. It's the only way the dealer can keep track of the ownership of bets.

If you're standing along the front of the table, for example, the come bet will be moved to the front of the point box corresponding to your position at the table. If you're standing along the end of the table, your come bet will be moved to the back of the point box. Think of the boxes as having four chip positions along the front for the four potential players along the front of the table, and four chip positions along the back for the four potential players along the end of the table. Incidentally it's a good idea to keep an eye on your bets in the point boxes. Don't rely on the dealer to keep all the bets straight.

ODDS ON THE COME BET

Since the come bet is just like the pass-line wager, you can take odds on the come bet too—and you'll definitely want to do that. To make the all-important odds bet on a come bet that went to a point box, simply position the bet (you know the routine) in that section of the come area nearest to your position at the table. That's right—in the same spot where you made your come bet. While doing this, announce to the dealer loudly and clearly, "Odds on my come bet." Otherwise, the dealer might think it's another come bet you're making. You see, after a point number has rolled, the dealer will have already picked up your come bet and placed it in the point box. It's the first action of a dealer on rolled point numbers: Placing all come bets in their proper point box location. When the come bet and odds bet are repositioned in the point box, the dealer places your odds bet on top of the come bet, but offset slightly to distinguish the odds bet from the come bet.

When the shooter repeats a come-bet point for you, the dealer will immediately return your come bet and odds bet to the come area where you originally placed them. Next, the dealer will place your winning chips directly beside the bets. Again, if you don't pick up all the chips, they work on the next roll as another come bet. Be careful!

Let me repeat an important aspect of what you've just learned: When you make a come bet and odds bet, always be sure to position the bets in the come area near the perimeter of the come area and in direct line with where you're standing. Don't just throw your chips down or place them anywhere in the come area. Your bets may later be confused with another come bet placed by another player. It's your responsibility to keep track of your own bets. There's always some jerk at the tables who thinks your chips are his chips.

OFF AND ON

Let's say you have a come bet on 6, and decide to make another come bet so that you can have two come bets in action. You make the bet, and the shooter throws your 6. If the come bet you just made and the come bet sitting in the point box are of the same value (not counting odds), the dealer will simply pay your winnings beside the come bet in the come area instead of moving the chips about. Pick up your winnings and let your new come bet stay there awaiting another roll.

If the come bets are not of the same value, it could be confusing to figure out the net winnings. Never let a dealer do this! Insist that the come bet with odds that has just hit is paid, and the new come bet is moved to the same box awaiting your new odds bet, essentially creating a new bet.

OFF ON THE COME OUT

You can remove your odds bets at any time, or simply call them "off" whenever you like, on a whim or whatever, but there's no particularly good reason for doing that. Of course, you can't remove a pass-line bet or come bet. Otherwise, you would have a healthy advantage by just letting the bets work on the come-out roll (where you have a big advantage) and then simply taking the bets down if a point number is established (where the edge swings to the casino). Obviously, the casinos won't go for that! But since the odds bet is fair with no advantage either way, casinos will let you do as you please with it.

However, casinos have a standing rule that all odds bets are automatically off on the come-out rolls unless you say otherwise. The theory is that most players don't want to lose the odds bets in case a 7 is rolled on the come-out, which would wipe out all the come bets in the point boxes. The 7 does in fact wipe out your come bets—but with the odds called off, the dealer will return all your odds bets to you. It's a standard house rule, so go with it.

THE POWER OF COME BETS ON BIG SHOOTS

The best reason I can give you for making come bets with odds is to gang up on the table when a shooter is repeating a lot of point numbers that would otherwise be useless to you if you were just betting the pass line. Don't let all those beautiful numbers go to waste! That's your cue to make a come bet or two. But as we discussed, in the case of multiple odds, don't go overboard on come bets either. And, like multiple odds, you can use come bets as a form of a betting progression. Start out by just betting the pass line. If you win a few bets, make a come bet. If you continue winning, make another.

When a shooter is on a roll, I might have as many as three come bets working for me. When one hits, I start another one so that I always have three bets in the boxes. When the inevitable 7 clears the table, and I lose my come bets, I go back to my basic pass-line-only status and wait for another streak of wins before I begin launching come bets again.

PLACE BETS

For players who are too anxious to get their money on the table, especially on their favorite point numbers, casinos allow bettors to **place** any or all of the point numbers without having to go through the rigmarole of waiting for them to come up as a come-bettor must do. But for this luxury, you have to pay a price. Certainly the casino won't pay true odds as they do on your odds bets. No way!

Here's a schedule of how the casino pays place bets.

PLACE NUMBER	ODDS PAYOFF	SHOULD BE	CASINO ADVANTAGE
6 & 8	7 to 6	6 to 5	1.52%
5 & 9	7 to 5	3 to 2	4%
4 & 10	9 to 5	2 to 1	6.67%

Placing the 6 or 8 is not a bad bet at all, only a meager 1.52 percent house advantage. Occasionally, I'll catch myself placing a 6 or 8 if the number is not covered with a come bet. Still, the casino edge is two and one half times greater than a pass-line bet or come bet with double odds. But don't let that stop you if you want to make place bets because the 6 or 8 place bets are the most likely place bets to streak. In the event that you do place a 6 or 8, be sure to make your wager in multiples of $6 because the payoff is 7 to 6. For example, if you bet $30 on the 6, the payoff is $35.

Dealers position place bets in the point boxes in a similar fashion to come bets. However, you must tell the dealer what the bet is that you want to make. It's not a big deal, so you don't have to carry on a conversation. If you want to bet $6 on the point of 8, simply say, "Six-dollar 8."

ONE-ROLL BETS

There are many popular one-roll bets known as **proposition** bets where you either win or lose on the next roll. Perhaps the most popular bet is simply known as **eleven**, also affectionately called "**yo**." The most popular time to bet eleven is on the come-out roll. The house advantage on this wager is a little over 11 percent, which makes it easy to remember, right? Eleven percent for number eleven!

In spite of that high percentage, it amazes me how many dice players make this wager, including those who should know better—like me. May I offer a brief story?

FOUR ROLLS: THREE THOUSAND DOLLARS!

My two friends had been playing craps for hours when I joined them. They looked tired and beaten. The friend whom I worry about the most, the one who just loves to play, had lost nearly all of his bankroll. My other friend, who is newer to the game, was barely holding on, literally, with his few remaining chips clutched tightly in his hands. He was taking cues from "All Nighter," as I jokingly call my other friend, learning bad habits that would surely send him home early. I decided it was time to pull him away.

I didn't like the looks of the table, the players, or anything else about this moment except one very vital thing: I liked the roar that erupted like a waking lion when the shooter made his point. At the far end of the table, this new player, who had just walked up about the same time I did and was promptly handed the dice, had breathed new life into the game. The timing couldn't have been better!

I had a few hundred in my pocket, and one straggler green chip ($25 chip) that I had missed when I had cashed in several hours earlier—and from this same table, incidentally, a table that had looked a lot better in the morning than it did now, stretching every single chip from the players like a torturer's rack. But there was change in the air. Like the lull before the storm, you could feel it.

A nod of assurance to both of my friends was all I needed to do. But in case they didn't get my signal, I tossed that green chip on the table and told the dealer on the stick, "Eleven." He looked at me as though he wondered if I knew what I was doing. I didn't have a bet on the pass line, and he quickly pointed that out to me.

"Eleven, you said, right?"

"All of it," I said, as if it were a $500 chip and they needed something in writing. If there's such a thing as a perfect eleven, this dapper new shooter threw it! Nice and easy, nice and sweet.

"Three-seventy-five right here," says the stickman as he taps the butt end of his stick on the table in front of me, authorization in triplicate for the dealer to pay me three blacks ($100 chips) and three greens.

"Seventy-five dollars here, and to this gentleman too," he says, tapping the table in front of my friends who had each snuck a nickel chip ($5) on that same lucky number. Lucky? No, it had nothing to do with luck. It was all a matter of timing—and it wasn't over.

"Press it up," I said, as I threw another green chip to the stickman and placed two green chips on the pass line.

"Eleven," says the stickman, "Yo-o-o 'leven!" as the shooter rolled it again. It was easy for me to bet this guy with the dice.

"Press it again," I said and placed two more green chips on the pass-line.

"Eleven again!" says an astonished stickman. Now the table's catching on. Everyone's on 11!

It hit again! And I calmly collected nearly three thousand dollars on four rolls of the dice. And four rolls of the dice would be it for me: I left before my friends even knew I was gone. The storm was over, and I knew All Nighter would have his work cut out for him, with a lot of money to shovel back to the casino. I included this story because I want you to know that sometimes these high percentages will unleash their high payoffs, raining chips all over the players. If you listen closely enough, you can hear the "wins" start to blow.

ACES & TRAINS

The two other popular one-roll bets are **aces** (2) and 12. There is only one way to make either of these bets: You have to see one dot on each die for aces, and a trainload of dots on the dice for a 12!

These two bets torment dice players more than any other. Rarely does a player bet them both; it's usually one or the other. And you know what that means, right? If you bet aces, the **train** (12) pulls in. If you bet the train, two little dots will laugh in your face. The solution, of course, is to bet them both—but again, you know what will happen, right? You'll see one die with one dot and the other die with six dots. Okay, so it's a 7, but at least you won the pass line.

When I see players betting 2 or 12 or both, I tell them to take those bets over to the roulette table where they can make essentially the same wagers for a heck of a lot less percentage. Here's the way it plays out:

| | CRAPS | | ROULETTE | |
BET	PAYS	TRUE ODDS	PAYS	TRUE ODDS
2 or 12	30 to 1	35 to 1	35 to 1	37 to 1
2 & 12	15 to 1	17 to 1	17 to 1	18 to 1

You are paid more at the roulette wheel because the percentages are better! Compare nearly 14 percent at the dice tables to a little over 5 percent at the wheel. Technically, there are two more numbers in the mix at the roulette table, 38 versus 36, but that is more than made up for in the payoffs.

And now, how about the 11 at the dice tables? Following the same idea as our 2 and 12 bets above, let's say the 11 is bet for $5 at the dice table. If it hits, the payoff is $75 (15 to 1). Now, let's take that $5 to the roulette table and bet only $2 of it on 11. If it hits, the payoff is $70! If it doesn't hit, you can do it again and still have a buck left in your pocket! Oh, go ahead, put the buck on 11—if it hits, you win $35. That nickel gives you three shots at the roulette wheel (okay, two and a half) versus one shot at the dice tables.

Yes, I know: The 11 at the dice tables is technically two numbers (5-6 and 6-5) if we are to compare them to roulette numbers. We're comparing two numbers out of 36 to one number out of 38. But let's not get too picky about it: It's still worth your consideration from a pure percentage standpoint.

HARDWAYS

You can't write a book on casino craps without at least a cursory discussion of **hardways**. Cursory, indeed: That's usually about all the ink they get. You see, hardways have a dubious distinction among many gaming authors (my earlier writings included) of being nothing more than sucker bets. It's exactly what you should expect from the math wizards (this author *not* included) who worship percentages as some sort of fringe religion. "It's all percentages," they say, "so just go with the percentages." I guess you're supposed to forget that we are all creatures of chance, and that we all like to take one every once in a while. I think it's called gambling.

And to make gambling just a bit more personal, we all like to test our own intuitions, to stare down the percentages and see if we can make them blink. Go ahead and play the game "by the book" if you like, and have fun. Without hardways? You must be kidding! Among the monster wins I've experienced at this roller-coaster game, hardways have been instrumental in all of them! Yes, I said *all* of them!

For those who are new to the game, let me tell you all about these bets. **Hardways** are simply the point numbers 4 or 10 and 6 or 8 made in pairs, such as 2 and 2 for the 4, or 3 and 3 for the 6. Any other ways to make point numbers are called **easy**, such as 5 and 1 for the 6.

BET	PAYS	SHOULD PAY	CASINO ADVANTAGE
Hard 6 (or 8)	9 to 1	10 to 1	9.1
Hard 4 (or 10)	7 to 1	8 to 1	11.1

Look at the payoffs for hardways and note that the 6 and 8 hardways pay the same, as do the 4 and 10 hardways, but the 6 and 8 hardways pay more than the 4 and 10 hardways and even sport a slightly lower percentage. The reason they pay more is because there are more "easy" ways to make them. In other words, there are more ways to lose the bet, since hardways lose when they're made the easy way. So, if there are more ways to lose, they should pay more, and they do. The hardways 6 and 8 pay 9 to 1. The hardways 4 and 10 pay 7 to 1. That's the opposite of what most rookie players would expect because they know that the 4 and 10 point numbers are harder to make, so they just expect the 4 and 10 hardways to pay more too. But as I've just explained, they are misguided in their reasoning.

The dealer places hardway bets at the center of the table. Simply toss your bet to the dealer and announce, "Five-dollar hard 6." The bet is placed in a box that, unlike the point-number boxes, represents the whole table, not just one end. So, to find your spot in the box, you first have to mentally divide the box in half. If you're standing beside the dealer just left of center, your spot in the box is the left corner formed by the front edge of the box and that invisible line you drew that divides the box. Don't worry, you'll catch on!

Since hardways win when point numbers are made in pairs, if you're on the hard 6, you need a 3-3 to win. Any other 6— and there are four of them (1-5, 5-1, 2-4, and 4-2)—will lose the bet. Of course, a 7 will also lose the bet, and it doesn't have to be a seven-out. In most casinos, "Hardways work unless called off" is a standard cry of the dice dealers. That means you'll lose your hardway bets with a 7 on the come-out roll. So do as I do and call your hardways off on the come-out. It helps you relax.

I feel that I must tell you this one more time because it's tough to preach against the odds: Hardways really shouldn't be encouraged, no more than 11 or 2 or 12. But if you like to buck the odds, as I do, go ahead and experiment with them on a conservative basis. Make up your own mind and see what you think, but remember what else I told you earlier: In all my years of having a love-hate relationship with this game, there were times when I wanted to go out and buy red roses for this capricious lady, in appreciation for parading her numbers in pairs.

An old friend of mine from the dice pits of yesteryear used to call these lovely pairs "identical twins." And he's right—they double your pleasure and double your fun! In fact, hardways became such a passion for me that I developed my own strategy for playing them. It's not complicated, so let me tell you about it right here, right now.

To help take the edge off the percentages, I only bet hardways with winnings from other bets. For every $30 in winnings, I toss a nickel chip on either the 6 or 8. If the bet

CRAPS: HOW TO WIN

wins, I **press** it, which means that I double it. Every time it wins, it gets pressed. The idea, of course, is to build the stack.

I like to think of my hardway bet as a bomb that I'm building. And as my winnings accumulate from other bets, I take a little of that gun powder and add it to my bomb. The anticipation of that bomb blowing up in the casino's face is most exciting, even if it's just a small one! But sometimes I can build it up to well over $100 and hope that the Fourth of July comes early. Sure, sometimes the bomb fizzles. Then I have a decision to make as to whether or not I restore the bomb to its full pack, or start from scratch, or just wait. Those of you who want to build your own bombs can design that part of the strategy for yourself.

A reader wrote to me a while ago and told me he liked the idea of building up one bet with winnings, but chose to do it as a *buy bet* on the 4 or 10 instead. **Buying** the 4 or 10 is just like placing it as a place bet, but you pay a five percent commission to get true odds. If his bomb explodes he gets 2 to 1, not as exciting as 9 to 1, but his explosions will be more frequent than mine. The percentage on the 4 or 10 buy bet is 4.76 percent, so he's smarter in that respect. And, frankly, it's an interesting twist on my "building the bomb" strategy. (The mention of buy bets reminds me that I haven't covered all the bets you can make at a dice table, but there's really no reason to make this book some sort of craps encyclopedia, as that is not its thrust.)

THE "LADY'S BET"

There are so many variations on the one-roll **field bet** today that I can't give you the specific percentages. Let's just say around 4 to 5 percent. It's a tempting bet to the uninitiated because there are so many field numbers that win, although there are more ways to lose, of course. Suffice it to say that in the days before women really caught on to craps, all they made were field bets, so it became known as the "lady's bet." If a woman asked a craps dealer (all male in those days) for a little assistance, the dealer would show her the big box on the layout marked FIELD. "Put your bet right here, young lady, and if any of those numbers come up, you win."

That's craps? No, that's not craps—that was just a brush off.

DON'T PASS, DON'T COME, AND DON'T GET EXCITED

The sections of the table layout marked DON'T PASS and DON'T COME are for betting with the casino and against all the other players, assuming they're not all making don't bets too. Technically, don't bettors are not betting with the casino, but they do win when the casino wins, except in one case: When a 12 is rolled on the come out, the don't bettor doesn't win; it's a **push** (a standoff). The percentages are about as small as the "right" side (betting the dice do pass) and the BAR 12, as the push is called, is worth the 1.40 percent house edge.

The only problem with the don't bet is that you want a cold table in order to win. You win when the other players lose. You're siding with the enemy. I never play the don't side because it's too darn boring. No excitement. And there shouldn't be. It could be dangerous! Don't bettors should never yell and scream and wave their arms when a shooter sevens out. Even though they have won, other players might have lost thousands! Winning on the don't side with even a smile of arrogance on your face will get you looks that could kill, so be sure a security guard is handy if you plan on touting your win to the other players. However, if you're the type who likes to antagonize other people, the don't bets were designed just for you!

HIDING THE PERCENTAGES

Those who know me and play beside me know that I like the long-odds bets, whatever and wherever they are. Any game. Any team. Any horse. The price I pay for these bets is almost always a higher percentage, because casinos like to hide their higher percentages in the higher payoffs.

If you win a few dollars on an even money bet, the casino usually won't take much out for itself. But if you win a few hundred dollars on a high-odds bet, the casino takes a bigger bite. The idea is that you won't notice it as much when a big payoff is pushed in front of you. Like I said, they hide the bigger percentages in the big-money payoffs. Which reminds me: When I win a big payoff, I do not hide my excitement. It's why I play. I play for the anticipation of a big win, and when it comes, if it comes, it seems perfectly natural to me to express excitement. I have always been suspicious of those who show no enthusiasm when winning.

Enjoy the game, but go easy with it. And if you decide to build bombs as I do, learn how to build your excitement too. And show it—never hold back!

6   BLACKJACK: HOW TO WIN!

Do you know the worst possible move at a blackjack table? I'll bet you don't! The worst possible move you can make is to walk up to any table with a seat open, sit down and start playing. It's the wrong thing to do for two reasons. First, shrewd gamblers always watch a table for a few minutes, or a few more minutes, for as long as it takes, to make sure they're not walking into an ambush. Watch first, play later is true of any game, not just blackjack.

But this mistake is doubly dumb at a blackjack table, which leads us to mistake number two. Blackjack is not a constant, negative-expectation game. The percentages are always changing as cards are played. A player who keeps a count of the cards knows where the percentages are at any given moment. Logically, it would make no sense at all to just sit down and play when you have this weapon available to you—a weapon that can tell you when to play and when not to. Clearly, you should sit down and play only when the count is favorable. If you don't fully understand what I mean by the "count," you will soon enough.

Technically, there's a third reason why you should never walk up and take a seat, although it's becoming less and less of a reason as the game becomes more standardized. There are still venues where variations in game rules are worth looking for. In those cases, it would behoove you to ask about the game rules before you play. If you don't like what you hear, move on to another casino in the market. Then ask again. In fact, ask around. The rule variations in some major markets are so severe that the simple act of finding the most player-friendly rules is worth a good point, maybe two points, against the percentages. Before you've finished this chapter, you'll know the rules to ask about. Specifically, you'll know which rules often vary, and thus are responsible for the biggest swings in percentages.

THE OBJECT OF THE GAME

Blackjack is played with a standard deck of 52 playing cards like the ones you can buy in any drugstore, but with the jokers removed. You and any other players at your table (up to seven) are playing against the casino, represented by a **dealer** who merely deals the cards and has no other vested interest in the game. The dealer's actions are mandatory, based on strict game rules. Technically, a machine could deal the game, since no game skill is required.

The only possible dealer "skill" to worry about is cheating, but it happens very rarely if ever, especially at the larger, well-known casinos. Many years ago, cheating might have been a problem, but today, with the priceless value of a gaming license and the casino's ability to generate substantial income honestly, cheating is an inconceivable enemy.

It's wrong to think of the dealer as your adversary, as many players do. Dealers are not trying to beat you unless you have antagonized them in some way. Other than intentionally short-paying you, there is really nothing dealers can do in the course of performing their job that could hurt your chances of winning. Your real adversary in the game is, of course, the casino. As in all casino games, the casino wants to win your money. You want to win the casino's money. I would call that an adversarial relationship, and I think it's important that you understand that going in.

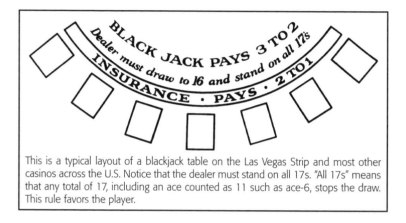

This is a typical layout of a blackjack table on the Las Vegas Strip and most other casinos across the U.S. Notice that the dealer must stand on all 17s. "All 17s" means that any total of 17, including an ace counted as 11 such as ace-6, stops the draw. This rule favors the player.

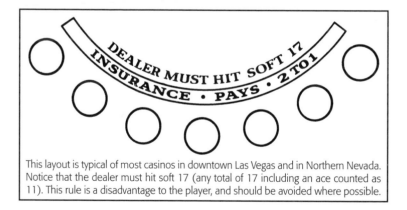

This layout is typical of most casinos in downtown Las Vegas and in Northern Nevada. Notice that the dealer must hit soft 17 (any total of 17 including an ace counted as 11). This rule is a disadvantage to the player, and should be avoided where possible.

THE BASICS

Cards are dealt from a **shoe** (a box containing more than one deck) or by hand to the player and the dealer, each getting two cards. One of the dealer's cards is dealt face up for everyone to see, while the other is placed face down. The simple object of the game is for the player to have a **hand** that totals 21, or is closer to 21 than the dealer's hand.

The number cards count as face value, the **picture cards** (kings, queens and jacks) count as 10, and the ace is counted as either 1 or 11, whichever is better to make or approach 21. The four suits have no significance in blackjack; only the number value of each card is used. For example, if you are dealt a 6 and a queen, your count is 16; if you have two queens, your count is 20.

HITTING, STANDING, BUSTING

If you're not satisfied with your first two cards, you may ask the dealer to **hit** your hand with an additional card, or with as many as you like until you **stand** (are finished). If you take too many cards and exceed 21, it's an automatic **bust** and you immediately lose. Toss your cards on the table between the betting area and the dealer, indicating the bust. The dealer will remove your wager. In most casinos today, all of the cards dealt to players are placed face up so that you never need to touch the cards, and shouldn't. When you bust, the dealer will remove your cards (and your wager) for you.

When all players at the table have acted on their hands, the dealer turns over his **hole card** (the card dealt face down) and stands only if the total is 17 or more. The dealer is required to draw cards until the hand totals at least 17 or more. If the dealer busts in the process, all players who did not bust are automatic and immediate winners.

If the dealer does not bust and has a hand that totals between 17 and 21 (which it must, because the dealer draws to make at least 17, and anything higher than 21 is a bust), the hand is compared to yours to see which is closer to 21. Whichever is closer, wins. If both you and the dealer have the same total, it's called a **push** (a tie) and there's no decision on the bet. In that case, you are free to remove your wager, increase it, or decrease it. Only after a push or after a win can you again touch the chips in your betting area. Never touch your bet after a game has begun and before the hand is settled. Casino personnel are very suspicious.

Read this brief section again carefully until you fully understand it. It's the essence of the game! If you're wondering about which hand totals to draw cards, or at what point to stop drawing, don't worry about it now. We'll cover that later, at precisely the right time, for all possible hand combinations.

PAYOFFS, BLACKJACK, INSURANCE

All bets that win are paid at 1 to 1 odds (**even money**). If you bet $5, you win $5, and so on. However, if your first two cards are a 10-value card and an ace, it's called a **blackjack**, which wins outright and is paid at 3 to 2 odds (6 to 5 in some games). If you bet $10, you'll receive $15 in winnings! The 10-value card does not need to be a picture card. A 10 of spades or any other suit is worth just as much as a king, queen or jack. Any 10-value card and an ace make a blackjack. If the dealer receives a blackjack on the first two cards, you lose at even money (only the amount of your wager) unless you also have a blackjack, in which case it's a push.

The only other exception to the even-money wagers is called **insurance**. Here's how it works: If the dealer's upcard is an ace, the dealer will ask all the players if they wish to take insurance. To do that, you must bet an additional amount up to one-half of your original wager. You're betting that the dealer does, in fact, have a 10-value card underneath, in which case your side bet wins at 2 to 1 odds. The bottom line on insurance is, don't do it! It's a silly bet that only increases the house percentage.

Some casinos today do not allow the dealer to peek at the hole card to determine if the dealer has a blackjack if an ace or 10-value card is showing. The peek is made before the players are given the option of taking more cards. But in some casinos the game is played out, and if the dealer does indeed have a blackjack, only your original bet loses (double down and split bets are returned to you) unless you also have a blackjack, in which case it is a tie. You lose against a dealer's blackjack even if you drew to make 21.

> Insurance is a bad bet that increases the house percentage.

The reason that some casinos no longer allow peeking at the hole card is to discourage collusion between a dealer and a player who are attempting to cheat the casino. A dealer could signal the hole-card value to a player and thereby give the coconspirator a tremendous advantage.

HIT OR STAND MOTIONS

To recap, the most important option you have is to either hit or stand. Your way of indicating to the dealer that you wish to hit or stand depends on whether the cards are dealt face up or face down. Although virtually all casinos today deal the players' cards face up, a few casinos still deal the players' first two cards face down, as was common many years ago, so I'll cover both scenarios.

At tables where the cards are dealt face up, you should never touch the cards. To signal a hit, you can make either of two motions. You can point at the cards, as I prefer doing, by actually touching the table with your finger about two to three inches from the cards. This way, there's no question that you want another card. Unfortunately, some casinos frown on this action for whatever illogical reason.

The other motion is to simply bring your hand toward you in a scooping motion. Be sure you do this over the table, so that the "eye in the sky" can see it to record. The casino's video cameras are there to protect both the casino and the player, with every table in fine focus. Don't be intimidated by them.

If you don't want another card, I recommend that you simply extend your hand toward the dealer as if to indicate "stop." The casino recommends a horizontal motion as if you're wiping a piece of glass above the table. However, it's been my experience that the wiping motion can easily be confused with the opposite signal, especially if a player is too sloppy with the motions. Try it my way—you'll like it!

At tables where the cards are dealt face down, you obviously must pick up the cards to read your hand. If you do not want another card, simply place both cards face down on the table and slide them slightly under your bet. In most casinos, it's all right to simply place the cards within close proximity of your wager. If you want a hit, keep the cards in your hand until it's your turn to play, and then lightly scrape the card edges toward yourself on the table.

Incidentally, it makes no difference whether the cards are dealt face down or face up in blackjack. This ain't poker! But it does make a significant difference if you're card counting, which we'll discuss later.

SPLITTING

Another important option for you is to **split** identical cards in your original hand, such as a pair of 8's. When this option is available, you do not just automatically do it! The decision to split or not to split your pair depends on whether or not it will be an advantage to you. When we get to our basic strategy later on, I'll detail each possible pair combination in comparison to the dealer's upcard, and tell you the optimum decision you should make.

For now, however, let's prematurely make two important rules abundantly clear: Never, never, never split 10-value cards, such as two face cards! And never split 5's or 4's. Always split aces and 8's! If you're an inexperienced player, see if you can quickly understand the solid reasoning behind these two important rules.

When you wish to split your cards at a face-down table, simply position your cards face up and behind your bet (to the dealer's side). Then make another wager of the same size and place it directly beside (not on top of) your original bet. At a face-up table, you only need to make a new bet inside the betting circle to indicate the split, since your cards are already in position.

Tell the dealer you wish to split the pair, and you will be given two more cards, one to each card you split, creating two new hands that are working for you. If you receive another identical card, some casinos will allow you to split again, and you'll have three hands in play. However, most casinos today do not allow the re-splitting of aces. To make matters worse, the hands stand after the dealer has given one card to each of the split aces. The casino will not afford you the option of hitting. Regardless, splitting aces is a strong player advantage. Always do it.

DOUBLING DOWN

Here's an option that figures significantly in your ability to adjust the percentages. You may **double down** on your first two cards by making an additional bet up to the amount of your original wager and receive only one card from the dealer. One hit.

Obviously, the time to double down is when you have a total of 10 or 11 and the dealer's upcard is 6 or less. That's the ideal situation. Another 10-value card will give you a 20 or 21. Even a 7, 8, or 9 will give you a pat hand (17 or better). That's the reason why I told you earlier to never to split 5's. The two 5-value cards give you a hand total of 10, and that's usually a good time to double down. I'll give you the complete basic strategy for doubling down and all the other player options later on, so that you'll know exactly when to do it, and when not to.

The casino industry has been negligent in its efforts to standardize game rules, as I've already mentioned. Perhaps the rules are an element of competition that shouldn't be standardized; but no matter: the rules do vary and doubling down is a good example. Some casinos limit double down to only 10 or 11. Still other casinos will allow double down on any two cards, and that's a big advantage to the player. Unfortunately, most casinos not only have different rules, they change their rules about as often as the cost of gasoline goes up, so the best solution is to simply ask before you play.

SURRENDER

Surrender is an option that few players understand or readily use, probably because many casinos no longer offer it. If you are fortunate to play in a casino where surrender is available, this is what it means to you: If you don't like your first two cards—and that happens a lot—you can surrender the hand and lose only one-half of your bet. Simply say, **Surrender!** to the dealer and throw in your cards. The dealer will remove half of your bet, and you're out of the woods. It's that simple.

There was a time when I refused to play blackjack in any casino that didn't have surrender rules. Who wants to hit a 15 or 16 against the dealer's 10? Years ago, a player could surrender before the peek—the casinos called it **early surrender** and they promoted it wildly to attract players. The rule was rather rudely downgraded in later years to **late surrender**, where a player could only surrender after the peek. Suffice to say, casinos today are getting all the players they need without it!

A SOFT HAND

Any hand that includes an ace has two values—a soft value and a hard value. If your hand is an ace-6, the **soft** value is 17 (counting the ace as 11), and the **hard** value is 7 (counting the ace as 1). Although it doesn't come up that often, you must decide whether or not to hit a soft 17 or 18. A soft 19 or 20 is good enough and you should stand.

A soft hand such as a soft 17 will not bust. Getting hit with a 10-value card will simply turn a soft 17 into a hard 17. Depending on the dealer's upcard, you actually may want to double down on a soft 17, if the casino allows you to do it. I'll give you the basic strategy for soft hands in the following pages.

Earlier in this chapter, I told you that the dealer is required to draw to 16 and stand on 17. That's the basic rule on the Strip in Las Vegas and in most other major casinos across the country, but the rules are different in many casinos in Downtown Las Vegas, Northern Nevada, and some Indian casinos, where the casino requires the dealer to hit a soft 17. It's a nasty ploy and definitely a disadvantage to the player. So before you play, look at the table layout, which should clearly state, "The dealer must draw to 16 and stand on *all* 17's." Much better!

BASIC STRATEGY

Before we look at the strategy charts, let's apply some good old-fashioned horse sense and see if we can understand the reasoning behind them. You'll be able to remember the strategies more easily if you understand why they work.

First, let's identify the potential bust hands as **stiffs**—and that's a great term for them. When the dealer gives you a hard, unpaired 12, 13, 14, 15, or 16, you got stiffed! If your hand is 15 or 16 (other than 8-8), you've got one of the two worst hands possible—and it's especially tough if the dealer's upcard is a 7 or higher. Don't screw it up any more than it already is by not hitting it, or by not surrendering if the rules allow you to do that.

If your cards total 17, 18, 19, or 20, you have a **pat** hand, decent enough. Although 17 and 18 may be good enough to stand on, they certainly won't get all the marbles all the time. Blackjack, 20 and 19 are the real goodies you're looking for.

> Making the player draw before the dealer is the house's biggest advantage in blackjack.

WORKING THE PERCENTAGES

Judging by what we now understand to be the object of the game and the basic game rules themselves, it would appear that the biggest casino advantage is the fact that the player has to draw before the dealer does. That simple fact accounts for a hefty 7 percent advantage to the house. Sensing that problem, many inexperienced players elect to never hit a stiff for fear of busting. That dumb little ploy is worth about 3 percent to the house. We can work their 7 percent advantage down in other ways, but not that way. Read on!

Many casinos that offer a single-deck game are now paying only 6 to 5 for a blackjack, while most casinos dealing a double deck or 6- and 8-deck shoes have retained the 3-to-2 payoff. If you don't get 3 to 2 for a blackjack, don't play! The 3-to-2 payoff reduces the house advantage from 7 percent to a little under 5 percent.

Further, player options based on basic strategy—including hitting, standing, doubling, and splitting for both hard and soft hands—will lower the house percentage to about 1/2 percent. This number cannot be determined precisely because of variations in rules from one casino to another, and the frequent rule changes that occur. In addition, a multiple-deck game will add at least 1/2 percent to the casino's edge, regardless of the player's skill. Mediocre strategy may give the casino another 2 to 3 percent advantage, and a poor strategy may increase the casino's edge to 5 percent or more! Multiple-deck games will affect the percentages and the strategies presented in the next section, but only to a limited degree. However, it can be concluded that multiple-deck games are indeed an advantage to the casino, not to the player!

THE GOOD CARDS AND THE BAD CARDS

Now, let's see if you can identify the "good" cards and the "bad" cards for the player. Think about it, it's important. It would seem obvious that all 10-value cards are good, because they help give you 20, and they pair up nicely with an ace for a blackjack. Sure, 10-value cards are good!

But what about 2, 3, 4, 5, and 6? They help to promote those lousy stiffs, right? And more importantly, they can improve a dealer's stiff hand. Indeed, 2, 3, 4, 5, and 6 are bad cards!

Although we're getting a little ahead of ourselves, the object of card counting is to determine how many 10-value cards and how many small cards are left in the deck, based on how many you've seen played. When the ratio of 10-value cards to small cards is high, you have an advantage. If there are too many small cards left in the deck, the casino has a distinct advantage.

The strategies that follow are very powerful, but understand that no strategy will help you win if you don't help yourself. Knowledge is power. But poor play on your part—reckless, senseless betting—can destroy that power in no time. Do yourself a favor. Read *What Casinos Don't Want You to Know*, a perfect complement to this book. The chapters on money management and commonsense betting will add a new, vital dimension to your game. The most powerful strategies in the world are useless to you if you aren't disciplined. Discipline is still the most powerful strategy of all!

Remember, you're going to play this game in commando-like fashion. These special commando forces win through unfailing discipline. They have it—you need it!

STRATEGY CHARTS

HIT-OR-STAND STRATEGY CHART FOR STIFFS

PLAYER'S HARD HAND	DEALER'S UP-CARD									
	2	3	4	5	6	7	8	9	10	A
16										
15			STAND					HIT		
14										
13										
12	HIT									

ALWAYS STAND ON 17 OR BETTER!

Our strategy for hitting or standing with stiffs is really quite simple, as you can see.

1. **Always hit a stiff when the dealer has a 7 or higher.** Remember it as 7-UP, and you'll never forget it.

2. **Always stand on a stiff when the dealer has a 6 or less showing, with the exception of 12.** The dealer does not have a pat hand (with the exception of ace-6), so there is a good possibility that the dealer will bust.

3. **Always stand on 17 or better.** Never, even in your wildest dreams, hit 17! Dealers must alert pit bosses in many casinos when a player hits 17 or better. See if you can guess why.

4. **Always draw a card on 11 or less.** You might actually double down or split depending on the card values, but at the very least, you'll always hit it.

Incidentally, the hit-and-stand rules apply not only to your original hand but to your hand at any time. For example, if your original hand is 10-4 against the dealer's 10, you hit it. You receive a 2. Now you have 16. According to the chart, you must continue hitting until you have 17 or better. Sure, the odds are against you, but you had a losing hand in the first place. Over the long term, you'll reduce the casino's initial advantage we talked about by about 2.5 percent with correct hitting and standing strategy. Reducing the percentages against you is the name of the game.

HARD DOUBLE-DOWN STRATEGY CHART

PLAYER'S HARD HAND	DEALER'S UP-CARD									
	2	3	4	5	6	7	8	9	10	A
11			D O U B L E							
10			D O W N							
9									H I	T

1. **You should always double down on 11**, regardless of the dealer's upcard.

2. **Doubling on 10 is restricted to a dealer's upcard of 9 or lower.** If the dealer's upcard is 10 or an ace, it's obviously too risky.

3. **Only double down on 9 if the dealer's upcard is 3, 4, 5, or 6.** Ironically, some experts differ on the rule for 9, but this is my position. Doubling down on 9 is a moot point in many casinos (especially Northern Nevada) where doubling is limited to 10 or 11. Doubling after you have split is equally restricted in many casinos. Ask before you play to be sure you understand the casino's rules—and always seek out the best playing conditions.

Using proper strategy for hard double downs (and for soft doubling, which I'll cover under "Soft-Hand Strategy") further reduces the casino percentage by about 1.5 percent. We're getting there!

SPLITTING STRATEGY CHART

PLAYER'S HAND	DEALER'S UP-CARD									
	2	3	4	5	6	7	8	9	10	A
A-A				S P L I T						
10-10				S T A N D						
9-9										
8-8			S P L I T							
7-7										
6-6										
5-5			D O U B L E							
4-4										
3-3	H I T		S P L I T					H I T		
2-2										

Most computer-aided strategies for splitting pairs are randomly defined with no symmetry to recognize, so it's exceedingly difficult for the layman player to remember. In fact, most errors in basic strategy are made when splitting. I've taken the liberty of simplifying the splitting strategy to make it much easier to remember, with only a minuscule tradeoff in accuracy.

Since the overall advantage to the player for correct splitting is less than 1/2 percent (the smallest of all the player options), you have no reason to be alarmed. The simplification of an otherwise complex strategy is justifiably appropriate for this text. Here's how to remember our special splitting strategy:

1. **Always split aces and 8's.**
2. **Never split 10's, 5's and 4's.**
3. **Treat 5-5 as 10 and follow our double-down rule.** Double if the dealer shows 9 or less, otherwise, just hit.
4. **Split 9's when the dealer has 9 or less.**
5. **Split 7's when the dealer has 7 or less.**

6. **Split 6's when the dealer has 6 or less.** Remember that the dealer's upcard is always the same or less than the card you're splitting with 9's, 7's, and 6's.

7. **Only split 3's and 2's when the dealer's upcard is 4, 5, 6, or 7.** Otherwise, just hit.

SOFT-HAND STRATEGY CHART

PLAYER'S SOFT HAND	DEALER'S UP-CARD									
	2	3	4	5	6	7	8	9	10	A
A-9 (20)										
A-8 (19)				S T A N D						
A-7 (18)										
A-6 (17)										
A-5 (16)										
A-4 (15)	H I T		D O U B L E					H I T		
A-3 (14)										
A-2 (13)										

Once again, our soft strategy has been ever so slightly simplified to make it easier for you to remember.

1. **Always stand on a soft 19 and 20.** They represent good hands, regardless of the dealer's upcard.

2. **Always double down (if it's allowed) on a soft 13 through 18 when the dealer has a 4, 5, or 6 showing.** Otherwise hit 13 through 17.

3. **With a soft 18, you have three options**, which makes it is the most difficult to remember.

4. **Always double down on a soft 18 when the dealer is showing a 4, 5, or 6.** Treat it just like you play the smaller soft hands.

5. **Hit a soft 18 when the dealer is showing a 9, 10, or ace.** With a 9 or higher upcard, the dealer may have a better hand, so it does pay to try to improve your soft 18. Remember, you can't bust any soft hand with a single hit.

6. **If you end up with a poor draw such as a 5 (hard 13), you must hit it again and take your chances.**

SURRENDER STRATEGY CHART

PLAYER'S HAND	DEALER'S UPCARD
15-16 (hard)	7-8-9-10-A

When you have the hands shown above under Player's Hand (15-16), surrender against the upcards shown in the second column, Dealer's Upcard.

Surrender is worth nearly one percent to you, so look for it (but don't expect to find it) in one-casino markets, as it is generally offered as a casino marketing tool in competitive venues, assuming there are empty tables to fill. The rules for surrender are simple:

- **Surrender a 15 or 16 stiff (except 8-8) when the dealer has a 7 or higher upcard (7, 8, 9, 10, A) if you're playing in a casino where it is allowed.**

Don't hesitate to lose half of your bet with a bad hand. It beats losing it all!

THE ADVANTAGES OF BASIC STRATEGY

Now that we have presented a solid basic strategy, it's important that you memorize the charts so that you'll know exactly what to do with every conceivable hand and dealer upcard. Don't guess. Follow basic strategy exactly! There's no reason to ponder.

Like anything else, our basic strategy charts will at first appear too complicated to memorize. But as you dig into them and practice, your skill should become second nature. Yes, your effectiveness will be measured by how much you practice! How well you are prepared will have a direct and lasting effect on your confidence level—and you know how important that is. Make a decision right now that you will faithfully practice. Get your own deck of cards and practice, practice, practice. Don't bet a dollar until you've mastered the strategy. It's really not that tough to master, and you'll develop a skill you can be proud of. The instant you see your cards, you'll know exactly what to do! You must have confidence in yourself before you can have any confidence in your game.

If the idea of memorizing all of the preceding charts does not thrill you, I have good news for you a few pages ahead. You'll be able to apply basic strategy *without* memorizing, although I recommend that you at least give it a fighting try.

What advantage does the casino have against a player who plays good basic strategy? I was hoping you wouldn't ask me that question!

Every gaming expert in the world has tried to come up with a nifty number, but no one can pinpoint it. Even with today's powerful computers, no one can give you a precise casino advantage because of the rule extremes that vary significantly from one casino to another. And even if you know the game rules in a particular casino, they are totally unstable and may change tomorrow!

Here are some questions to answer before you sit down at a table:

1. Is the game one-deck, two decks, or a multiple-deck shoe?
2. Does the dealer hit a soft 17?
3. Can I double down on any two cards?
4. Can I double after I split?
5. Can I resplit a pair?
6. Can I resplit aces?
7. Is surrender available?

Suppose we could find an exact percentage based on a certain set of rules (and we could if we wanted to), then what? Do you play a basic strategy absolutely perfectly? I doubt it. Are you mediocre? Probably. If you're a poor player, you'll give back most of the casino's 5 percent advantage or more. Do you see the point? No player is infallible.

To what degree do we correctly apply basic strategy? It's a significant question in determining the casino's edge.

LONG-TERM DECISIONS

Still another matter that you must consider when weighing the casino's percentage is the fact that it's built on long-term decisions. Nothing says the percentages can't vary by 10 percent or more during the short term! Incredible fluctuations can occur, especially with a single-deck game. Hopefully, all the big fluctuations will fall in your favor, but don't be so naive as to think you can't lose ten hands in a row. You can, and sometimes you will. There are no guarantees over the short term. You must understand this.

Using an arbitrary percentage of 1 percent (an acceptable number) only tells us that over a very long period, you will probably lose $1 for every $100 you bet. Betting $1 a hand, it would theoretically take 10,000 plays for the casino to win your $100. So, you can see that, although it is a very small number, 1 percent will wipe you out eventually. Don't be misled by little numbers!

I like to consider the casino advantage as being between 1 and 2 percent based on average playing conditions for an average player using basic strategy. My number is about as useless as any other expert's number, because of all the reasons we've just cited. But hear this: If an exceptional player finds a casino with exceptional game rules, blackjack can be considered a nearly even game. With surrender, the player may actually have a slight edge. With card counting, which you are about to learn, the percentage can swing to the player's side of the table even more.

Before we talk about card counting, I want to reinforce my point about percentages. Years ago, I got a big kick out of a leading expert's number for the casino percentage. He made a big deal out of it as if the media should report on his findings! Not to embarrass him, I'll change it a little but keep the same number of digits. He said that blackjack with basic strategy gives the house a .347 percent advantage. There's no qualification as to the particular game rules or to the accuracy of the player's performance, and why carry it out to three places? That's the ridiculous part. It's a totally useless, meaningless number, unless you plan on playing tens of thousands of hands under optimum playing conditions without making a single error in strategy.

TAKING THE STRATEGY ONE STEP FURTHER

What we can determine from our analysis, however, is that blackjack is about as safe to play as playing the pass line with full odds at the crap table, or even a stint or two at the baccarat tables. I'm not saying it's safe, mind you, I'm just saying it's about the same. Using basic strategy with 95 percent accuracy under decent playing conditions, I rate these games a toss up.

But hear this: If a player goes one step further and masters a count strategy to identify the fluctuations while they are occurring, blackjack is indeed a better game than craps. The tremendous advantage to keeping track of the cards is in increasing your bet size when the opportunity is there, and laying back when the opportunity is gone. Keeping track of the dice is a waste of time, as previous rolls have no effect on future rolls. But at the blackjack table, previous cards do indeed have an effect on future cards.

> Keeping track of the cards gives you the advantage of increasing your bet size when the opportunity is there.

COUNTING CARDS

Most gaming experts who have authored other books on blackjack steadfastly believe that you must keep a running track of all cards that have been dealt, follow an ever-changing basic strategy, and then adjust your betting for that rare moment (about 5 percent of the time) when the odds have shifted in your favor. In a nutshell, that's the computer-proven, mathematical approach to beating the game—but the method for counting cards that I'm going to show you is easier!

In order to keep an accurate count of the dealt cards, you must be able to concentrate fully. The casino won't let you drag in a laptop computer. Even a pencil and pad of paper are a no-no. To use the popular count systems widely advertised today, you simply must have a good memory recall, plus the stamina to stay with it. If you can't keep the count as you're supposed to, and you flat-out refuse to learn basic strategy, then blackjack will end up about a 5 percent game for the house or better. I'm just giving it to you like it is.

Blackjack is a unique game that requires two special skills. You already know about one of them—basic strategy. The other is counting. The professional player who might actually have a long-term advantage over the casino is a master at both. I'm going to give you the raw basics of a powerful counting strategy after we've learned why the strategy works. You must learn basic strategy first and really master it. Then when you're ready, you'll have the counting strategy ready to go. At least you won't have to go out and buy another book!

A REVIEW OF RULE VARIATIONS

Before we delve into card counting, let's go over some of the things we've learned regarding the game's fundamentals. Readers write to me on occasion and tell me about a casino where they've played that offers unusual rule variations. When I look into it, I find that "experiment" is a better choice of words. Here are five examples.

1. GIVING BONUS PAYOUTS

A common variation of the rules was introduced in the late '90s under several names, but they were all based on the same promotion—a bonus payoff to any player who made 21 with three 7's. Some casinos were more successful than others with this promotion. One casino on the Las Vegas Strip created a progressive jackpot that increased every hour. Score the three 7's and win the big jackpot!

Is this blackjack, or is this just some stupid gimmick? It's the latter, of course, a gimmick that has two purposes: (1) to lure players in by offering a bonus payout that most other casinos don't offer; and (2) to lure players in by offering a bonus payout that masks the game's otherwise unfavorable playing conditions. Invariably, these rule variations, or "side bets," as the casinos call them, are not an advantage to players. Be skeptical with these types of casino promotions.

2. OFFERING SURRENDER

On occasion, I'll find out that a special rule might be worth a player's attention. For example, now and then a few casinos reinstate surrender, but it's rarely offered anymore. Can you guess why? Even in hotly competitive markets, casinos have so many players that player perks are simply not required to fill the tables. An Indian casino in the Midwest that I monitored during the few weeks it offered surrender had a surprising result from its trial run. The intention was to test surrender and see if players took to it. In this particular market, there are six casinos all fighting over a regional and local market of players—no big airports, not even major interstate highways to bring in out-of-state players. So, this would be a typical case where a rule change might actually benefit the casino and the player. That's right: A player-favorable rule that obviously helps players and brings more players to that particular casino.

But the promotion was soon dropped. Why? I was stunned, but shouldn't have been, when the casino boss told me his reason for going back to the basic game. He said he installed surrender at four of his 16 tables, but players didn't flock to the surrender tables. Players didn't push and shove to get a seat at the surrender tables. Players didn't care which table they played at. Players, in fact, didn't know what surrender was! And although the casino made a valiant effort to educate its players as to the advantages of surrender, it seemed as if the players simply didn't care. Do you remember what I said in earlier about taking all the aces out of the decks on Saturday night? I rest my case.

3. DEALING THE CARDS FACE UP

Another change that seems to confuse players is whether or not cards are dealt face up or face down. The trend today has been to play the game only with cards up. The theory is that this policy will prevent players from touching the cards. Actually, it is to prevent certain players from marking the cards: "If you can't touch 'em, you can't mark 'em." But it would seem as if only those casinos with multiple decks (usually eight) play the game with the cards face up. As you'll soon learn, this is an important criterion for card counting, because having all the player cards face up makes counting much easier to do—and that probably explains why some casinos, especially those dealing fewer decks, choose to deal the cards face down.

4. PEEKING AT THE HOLE CARD

During the '90s, there was a trend among casinos to stop the dealer from peeking at the hole card if an ace or 10-value card was up, for reasons we discussed earlier in this chapter. It made every bit of sense, and many casinos still won't allow the dealer to peek. But that's changing again: It seems that without the peek, a game took longer to play. Furthermore, some players were upset when they fought their way to a 20 only to get beaten when the dealer turned over a blackjack. Casinos were putting the cart before the horse! And they were upsetting many of their players. So, today you'll find more and more casinos returning to what is affectionately known as the "peek rule."

5. DEALING MULTIPLE-DECK SHOES

Speaking of multiple decks, there's no question that the trend, particularly in states other than Nevada, is to fill up the shoe with eight decks. Casinos are convinced that a good card counter can't gain much from an eight-deck shoe because of all the cards left out of play behind the cut card. In some casinos, nearly two full decks are not allowed to go out and play. Pity the cards? No, pity the players! If the cards are not played, the casino's right: How could you count them? Most of the earlier counting strategies would be completely hogtied by this revolting development, but newer strategies such as the one you are about to learn mitigate these clever casino ploys.

Another disadvantage of multiple decks is the unusual drop in the frequency of blackjacks. The more decks in the shoe, the less blackjacks will appear. It's hard to explain, but it's all based on what mathematicians call dilution. Dilution affects players in more ways than producing a shortage of blackjacks: More decks tend to thin out fluctuations. In other words, more decks tend to keep the shoe running with a random distribution. Further, with more decks, there is less likelihood that small cards, for example, will clump together within the shoe. Card counters are looking for small cards (bad cards for players) to leave the shoe, and the sooner the better.

If you saw four aces removed from a hand-held single deck during the early deals, you can bet your bottom dollar that you won't see any more for the remainder of the deck. But if you saw those same four aces removed from an eight-deck shoe, their absence creates a much weaker effect from what you can garner about the remaining deck construction through card counting. There are certainly more aces left to be played. The effects of early anomalies in an eight-deck shoe are clearly not as dramatic as the effects on a single or double deck.

THE EVOLUTION OF BLACKJACK RULES

Although the game is standardizing, it's still an in-process evolution that will take a few more years to settle. My position is that the game will never standardize because of the new build up of competitive markets. You see, there is another dilution of sorts taking place across the country as more and more casino markets spring up and take players away from what were once

BLACKJACK: HOW TO WIN!

considered to be protected markets. The new markets are saying to the players, "So you don't like the game rules over there? Come over here. We have better rules to play by." And they do. The question is, for how long?

And there's another question that begs to be answered. In spite of the resurgence in roulette, not to mention the new players flocking to the craps tables and the countless slot players coming in busloads, blackjack has proven to be a venerable game. The question is, "Is it vulnerable?" The answer is still a qualified yes, but those of us who were fortunate enough to have played this game in the '60s would certainly like to turn back the clock. The game that was played then is not the game played today. But this is no time for nostalgia—we have to tackle the game as it stands today. And we will. In fact, we can apply many of the same principles today as then. However, what we also have to do now that we didn't have to do then is to avoid the casino's nasty countermeasures.

I know the game; you know the game. We both know that we must practice flawless basic strategy in our player options and add the element of card counting to give us a shot at long-term winning potential. Other than poker, there is no other table game in the casino that gives us a long-term shot for our money. That's right, blackjack is not always a negative-expectation game! Most of the time it is, but some of the time it isn't. A good card counter can detect those times when the edge has moved across the table—and for that fleeting moment, we've done something that other gamblers at other games can't do: We can predict opportunity.

GETTING AN EDGE

As far as basic strategy is concerned, it's not as tough today to apply it as it was years ago. Today we have strategy cards for all the casino games, which have been approved by nearly all casinos for players to use at the tables. A blackjack basic strategy card shows every dealer upcard and player-hand combination and tells you what to do. There is no guesswork.

Obviously, it's best to memorize the right moves, but let's be realistic. Some players are only occasional players. They can't be expected to remember all the player options and perform flawlessly during those twice-a-year trips to Vegas. Sure, strategy cards are a godsend, but I'm sure you're wondering why casinos allow their use. Simple: The cards speed up the games. There's no pondering, no hair twirling, no looking up to the heavens for help. It's all right there in front of you. There's absolutely no reason to slow down the game. Yes, casinos love these cards. Why? Because the more hands played, the more the casino makes! It's that simple.

I hope you don't think that all you have to do is get your hands on a good basic strategy card and you can tell your boss what he can do with your crummy job. Not quite! As good as these cards are, they are not going to wipe out all the casinos. With the way the game is being played today in virtually all venues, correct basic strategy will get the house percentage down to a little less than 1 percent to a nearly even game—but the casino still keeps its edge. What seems like a minuscule advantage is all the casino needs. Applied over time, tons of time, casinos crank out their profits from these token percentages to the tune of millions of dollars each month. More than that, the increased revenue the casino realizes from faster play more than offsets the reduced revenue from the use of strategy cards.

Card counting is the hallmark of any blackjack strategy. It's one of the few strategies that casinos actually fear. Knowing that played cards affect the distribution of future cards is the essence of card counting. If there were strategy cards for counting the cards, the casinos would not allow them. No chance! So don't bother looking for any. If you're going to do some fancy counting, you're going to have to do it in your head.

So why won't the casinos allow card-counting strategy cards? You can answer that one yourself. A good counter practicing basic strategy can take that minuscule percentage away from the casinos. Steal it right from under their noses, and then turn it against them. No, I don't think the casinos would be very receptive to that. But don't let the idea of having to do all this counting stuff in your head scare you away. Here's another example where more new ideas have popped up, based on older methods that were far too complicated.

THE IMPERIAL II COUNT STRATEGY

One of the neatest card counting strategies is what I call the Imperial II Count. It's a modernization of one of my earliest strategies that was based on an overview of played cards. It seems almost too simple to work, but it does! First, let me give you the basics behind the Imperial II Count so that you can understand the underlying principles. You'll be able to play it more efficiently if you understand how and why it works.

Most all casino blackjack tables today are played full or nearly so. Years ago, you could always find an open table and play the dealer heads up, and many of the older strategies, such as my original Imperial Count, were designed for just that situation. But it is become increasingly difficult to have a one-on-one confrontation with a dealer these days. Why? We can look to the airlines for the answer. How many planes fly full today? *All* of them! So, the casinos have decided to run their games with the same economics in mind. There are few if any open tables because open tables are not making money. On weekends, it's even tough to find open seats! The casinos have wised up and, like the airlines, now force their customers to play musical chairs. It seems as if every time you look for a seat, there are three available and four players who want them. Now, for a card counting strategy to be useful today, it must work at a full table of seven players—a perfect number for the Imperial II Count!

Another sign of the times is multiple-deck shoes. Outside of Nevada, your chances of finding a one-deck or two-deck game are slim and none, and slim just left town! Unquestionably, a good strategy today must be designed for multiple decks, particularly an eight-deck shoe. The good news is that eight decks is a perfect number for the Imperial II Count.

Virtually all multiple-deck games today are dealt with the cards face up. And that's an important consideration for card counting. How can you count them if you can't see them? Full tables, multiple decks, cards face up. So far, so good!

HOW THE IMPERIAL COUNT STRATEGY WORKS

Knowing that the small cards—2, 3, 4, 5, and 6—are bad cards for players, keeping a count of these cards, and *only* these cards, is the centerpiece of the Imperial II Count. The 10-value cards and the ace are the good cards for players, but we don't have to keep track of them because the Imperial II Count is a balanced count (five small-card values vs. five good-card values—A-K-Q-J-10). Keeping track of both good and bad cards would be redundant. The more small cards that are removed from the shoe the better. Ideally, the small cards should leave the shoe at a higher than normal exit rate, and that's what the Imperial II Count does: It measures the rate at which the small cards are played.

To make the Imperial II Count work best for you, always position yourself at third base, the seat, as you face the dealer, at the far left of the table (to the dealer's right), so that you can see as many played cards as possible before you act on your hand. If there are seven players at the table, you will see an average of 21 cards per deal—yours, all hits, and the dealer's upcard. Based on the ratio of small cards to all other cards, eight of these cards should be small ones. Simply count these small cards as you see them. If you count ten after the first deal, there's a slight player advantage. If you count six, there's a slight additional edge for the casino.

One obvious glitch in this strategy needs to be accounted for. The counting procedure I just outlined—looking for eight small cards out of a 21-card average—is based on the dealer's upcard being 7 or higher. If the dealer's upcard is one of the small cards you're tracking—2, 3, 4, 5, or 6—you must adjust your card average downward, accounting for fewer player hits, with the net result being that you will only be looking for seven small cards. The next paragraph explains this further.

The value of 21 cards per deal to seven hands is based on an average of 2.857 cards per hand when the dealer's upcard is 7 or higher, and 2.280 cards per hand when the dealer's upcard is 2 through 6. The values are based on actual casino studies. Computer models, based on perfect basic strategy and the widely used new standard for game rules, show these values to be somewhat higher. The deviations are most likely due to player-option errors resulting in lower hit frequencies. The numbers listed for "small cards" are simply the product of .3846 (small-card expectancy) and the cards-per-hand averages plus 1 (the dealer's upcard), times the number of players. The effects of rounded values should be negligible in the short term.

You need to make another adjustment if the table has exactly six players. With six players, when the dealer's upcard is 7 or higher, look for seven small cards. If the dealer's upcard is one of the small cards you're tracking, look for five more small cards. If the table has fewer than six players, avoid it. If the table where you're playing has six players and loses a player, move to another table with more players. Remember, you want as many players as possible in order to see as many cards as possible.

IMPERIAL II COUNT STRATEGY

DEALER'S UPCARD: 7 THRU ACE		DEALER'S UPCARD: 2 THRU 6	
# OF PLAYERS	SMALL CARDS	# OF PLAYERS	SMALL CARDS
7	8	7	7
6	7	6	6

KEEPING THE COUNT

Perhaps the neatest feature of the Imperial II Count is the way you actually keep a record of the rate of small cards appearing. I recommend using a chip as your means of recording the results. Choose a part of the chip's art work to act as an hour-hand, as if the chip is a clock face. Point the hand at 12 o'clock (straight up) to indicate a neutral count. As your count moves up in a favorable direction, simply turn the chip so that the hand is pointing to the right, perhaps at one o'clock. If the count is heading in an unfavorable direction, move the hand to the left.

The incremental turn of the chip is something you'll have to tweak for yourself. But it has to be relative to the degree with which you are seeing the small cards removed from the deck. Most of the time, you'll count the normal number of small cards for a particular deal, so you would not turn your chip. I only turn the chip a full hour's worth, for example, when I see a deal with a significant fluctuation from the norm, say three or four cards. I've played this new version of the Imperial Count for many years and I've never been in a position where the hand was pointing past five o'clock. Since the right half of the chip is positive and the left half is negative (so to speak), you should not move the hand beyond six o'clock.

USING YOUR NEW SKILLS

Just keeping the count is one thing—using it is another. So how do you use it? It's easy—simply use your count to adjust the size of your wagers. Make larger wagers when the count is player-favorable, and smaller wagers when the count is running against you. Again, I don't like making hard-and-fast rules about this, but the following chart should help you in structuring your wagers, though it should be used only as a guide.

BET AMOUNTS

NON-FAVORABLE			FAVORABLE		
COUNT	HAND	BET	COUNT	HAND	BET
0	NOON	TM	3	1 PM	2X
3	11 AM	TM	6	2 PM	3X
6	10 AM	EXIT	9	3 PM	5X

TM stands for Table Minimum.
Hand refers to the hour locations on a clock face.
Wager amounts show a bet-spread relationship only, and do not suggest specific dollar amounts. Wagers should never exceed the table minimum if values are not well within the right side of the clock. Change tables when the values have stagnated on the left side of the clock.

THE ADVANTAGES OF CARD COUNTING

You now know that card counting helps you by telling you when to bet more, when to bet less, and when not to bet at all. But did you know that it also helps you by telling you when to alter basic strategy? It's such an obvious feature that we really don't need a chart to explain it.

For example, if you are dealt a 10-6—a likely bust hand—and the dealer is showing 9, basic strategy says that you should hit that stiff. Ideally, you would like to know that an excess of small-value cards remains in the deck to be played. But what if your count indicates that there is actually a deficiency of small cards remaining? A deficiency of small cards most likely means an excess of 10-value cards. You certainly don't want a 10-value card in this case, so you alter basic strategy and stand instead of hit.

> The biggest advantage in using the Imperial II Count Strategy is that you only have to count forward.

The biggest advantage of the Imperial II Count Strategy is that you only have to count in one direction—forward. Older counting strategies require that you count both small and large cards, meaning that you would need to count forward as you see small cards and then count backward as you see large cards. Forward and backward. Up and down. Even from plus numbers to minus numbers. One, two, three, two, one, zero, minus one, minus two, minus one, zero, one, two, three, two, three, four, five, four, five, four, three, two, three, four and so on. "Hey!" you cry, "We get the picture!"

I played point-count strategies for many years before I devised the original Imperial Count. Point-count strategies were easy for me, but not for beginners; in fact, they weren't for many counters at all. They considered it work—and it took the fun out of playing for many who tried it. I remember teaching the game to a young medical student from India, a friend of mine who just loved blackjack. He had only started learning our language two years before we met, so his English was so-so. For him to actually count up and down would be like you or me keeping the count in letters instead of numbers. That's right, an alphabetical count—A, B, C, D, E, D, C, E, F, G, H, G, F. You try it! Try counting down the alphabet from G. Bet you can't do it in less than 20 seconds.

I should answer an e-mail question I received from several players shortly after the Imperial II Count Strategy was first published. In using the clock face as a gauge for keeping track of your count, I assumed that everyone would understand that the gauge doesn't reset after each deal. You begin the next round of cards with the gauge exactly where it was. That's the idea of using the gauge—to remember your number. The number, you recall, serves as an aid in setting the amount of your bet or in altering basic strategy, but some players wondered if they should reset the gauge after each deal. No, of course not! You only reset the gauge after a shoe has been played out.

MID-SHOE ENTRY

In theory, the count of the cards throughout a shoe should produce a balance of good cards and bad cards. That is to say, at the end of a shoe, your chip hand should be pointed toward noon. Of course, there's rarely a shoe in perfect balance because of the many cards that will be cut out of play. But for the sake of argument, let's say that a card counter found a substantially favorable condition late in the round as the cut card neared. Assuming that the counter had played through the shoe, the non-favorable experiences beforehand would have probably knocked him off his seat.

So what's the point? That's a good question. A card counter would have left early in the shoe, so there wouldn't have been any chance to play with the benefit of those missing small cards when the deck construction later changed. And in those more frequent cases where the shoe is running so-so, table-minimum wagers is about all that counters can do if they want to bide their time at the table. Most of the time, the cards are running in the middle, the "risk zone" as I call it. Players might as well be rolling the dice or pushing buttons on a video poker machine.

The smart move is to simply watch a game and jump in when the count is well into the "afternoon" range. Milk it and then jump back out when the count turns sour again. It's called mid-shoe entry, and let's just say that it's frowned upon by almost all casino bosses. In some casinos, you might not be allowed to play until the shuffle if you've been watching the game beforehand. Does this surprise you? You didn't think the casino was run by a bunch of stupids, did you? What a sight to behold: Tables full of card counters tying up precious seats, watching and waiting for the chance to drool all over the table. Not gonna happen! Not even if you're just standing around behind the players.

What to do, what to do? If you're really serious about mid-shoe entry, here's the solution. Engage the services of a confederate player to monitor the table through thick and thin. But this only works in some venues—some casinos will not allow gawkers to stand behind players. "Move on, buddy," you'll hear. Why? For the very reason I'm citing. This onlooker can signal a good table to the real player who's not in the vicinity of the pits. A simple cue will work. All the counter has to do is keep his eye on his confederate. When I was more active in this game (read: the good ol' days), my buddy would simply rub the back of his neck when the table was ready for me to attack. It worked well for many years—except once. Of all the times we played this charade, the one time it backfired is hard to forget. I saw the signal. I hurried over. I got clobbered!

"Why did you call me over here, for crying out loud?" I asked him.

"I didn't call you over."

"Yes, you did. I saw you rub the back of your neck!"

"Oh, yeah. I had an itch."

Playing the Imperial II Count with mid-shoe entry is dynamite! All you have to do is keep the count—and your chips—handy. You'll keep your risk to a minimum.

I always play blackjack using the only count strategy that is both the easiest and the most effective: the Imperial II Count. You should too. But you should also know that, as powerful as it might be, card counting has its limitations. Casino countermeasures are numerous. Deep cut-card penetration will take more than two of the eight decks out of play, greatly weakening the value of counting. Bet spreads are closely watched. Mid-shoe entry is often prohibited. And a premature shuffle will stop a counter cold, regardless of anything else.

Blackjack ranks a weak second to poker, the casino's top table game where you at least have a chance for long-term success. But I still treat blackjack with respect—hoping for a little respect in return, I guess.

7 TALES FROM THE TABLES

Allow me to close this book with some short stories and personal thoughts that might help you digest all that you have learned. Book knowledge is important, but actual experience is important too. Most of the anecdotes you are about to read are accounts of real adventures in casinos across the nation. Enjoy!

THE DESPERADO

My friend and I were in Vegas for a three-day gambling trip. Both of us won early when we first arrived. We played several short sessions, maybe a half-hour at the most for any one of them, and all with success. Our wins were substantial.

Later in the day, we tried it again, but with little success. I left quickly, deciding that I would wait until the next day to play again. I wanted to spend the rest of that day savoring the morning victory. Of course, I tried to pull my buddy away too, but he refused. He was in the process of giving back his morning win, and that did not put him in the best of moods. I knew exactly what he was doing: He could leave a winning table. He couldn't leave a losing table.

"I came here to play, John. Now let me play!"

"No!" I said. "With an attitude like that, you didn't come here to play, you came here to lose!"

"See ya."

"Yeah, I'll see you for dinner."

Dinner came and went when I found my friend still at the tables. It was like looking at carnage. All the winnings were gone, his cash bankroll was gone, and most of his marker account was also gone. All he had left were a few piddling chips in front of him. " I'll probably have to write that last marker for $500," he said. So I watched him, and he was right. He wrote it. And when that marker went bye-bye, he called his host over to the table and asked him to extend another $5,000. The host refused. He pleaded and begged. The trip wasn't over. He couldn't stand the thought of hanging around Vegas broke.

On my way to dinner earlier, I had stopped in to see his host, a personal friend, and had told him not to give my buddy any more credit. Hearing "no" from his host, my buddy looked at me with the same expression he probably had used so effectively as a kid to get anything he wanted. "What the hell am I supposed to do, John?" he asked.

The host looked at me. I looked at him. And we both, reluctantly, nodded yes. We knew full well that he was just going to lose it. The host told him that he was going to give him the $5,000, knowing that he was just going to lose it. It wasn't that he had read my mind, it was just that we both knew what was going to happen. He was right. I was right. My friend lost it all.

I have yet to see a winning session come out of desperation.

ROLLER COASTERS

The emotional high of winning big during a streak is equal in intensity to the depression of not winning much at all because you watched it go by. It's a hollow feeling when you think about how much you could have won. Don't let it happen! It brings a tear to my eye to see players betting a single red chip on each hand as they ride incredible streaks. And I've seen it happen too often: Instead of winning thousands, they win a few dollars.

Sometimes the streaks are not as evident as you might imagine. Many years ago in Las Vegas, I watched a shooter make 12 passes and a bunch of numbers along the way. For some reason, I jumped in late, but I still caught enough of it to make for a very successful trip. All the other players acted like zombies, making their token bets and collecting their token wins. When the shooter finally sevened out, a floorperson came over to me and just shook his head. "This table should have lost a hundred grand with a shoot like that. You know, John, that's how we pay for all this!" he said, motioning around the plush casino.

In that same casino that same evening, I witnessed a player string several wins together at the blackjack table. The rest of us were winning too, but not like this guy. We would all win on frequent dealer busts, but his wins were coming on strong hands also. The surprise to all of us is how long it took for him to realize what was happening. By the time he wised up and changed the color of his chips, his luck also changed.

The dealer didn't help matters much for this poor soul when she said, "You know, I think you just won 15 hands in a row. That might be some kind of a record. I'll check." Then she yells over to the boss in the pits about this guy's incredible run, signaling players and gawkers alike to zero in on our table just to see all the chips this guy had piled up. They came. They saw. All of $185!

Incidentally, if I am ever that fortunate at the blackjack tables, I'll ride up the streak with carefully determined increases regardless of how my count might be running. My betting progression for a streak of wins always takes precedence over whatever count strategy I might be using. In fact, nothing, absolutely nothing, will stop me from increasing my bets—unless, of course, my wife walks up to the table and asks me, "How are you doing?"

THE BATTLE OF LOGIC

Every morning would start the same for me during the days when I made frequent gambling junkets to Las Vegas. I got up early (jet lag, you know) and hit the gift shop for a newspaper to read during breakfast. On this particular morning it was very early, and the casino in the old Dunes Hotel was nearly empty. One craps table was going with just a few players. It so happened to be the table near the casino cage on the way to the gift shop.

I had no intention of playing: My schedule didn't call for rolling the dice at five in the morning, yet I was wide awake and precariously anxious. Know the feeling? Besides, it was really eight in the morning as far as my biological clock was concerned. The newspapers wouldn't be in yet, and I really wasn't that hungry. Are you getting the picture? I slapped my hand every time I reached for my wallet. Finally, I decided to just watch the action for a few minutes.

Here's what happened. A shooter would either throw a craps or a point number on the come-out roll. Another roll or two, then zap! Seven out. Line away. Pay the don'ts. I'm telling you it went on and on that way. The table was so cold that I remember every detail to this day—a dice table frozen in time (excuse the pun). I felt sorry for the players. Anyone who really wanted to play that morning had little chance. Remember, it was the only table open at that time of the morning, and who wants to walk across the street? Obviously, no one. Sure, a don't bettor could have cleaned up, but these guys were all right bettors like I am. As much as I enjoy winning, I would never enjoy winning by betting the don't pass line at a cold table, and I speak for many dice players.

Anyhow, I thanked my lucky stars that I didn't play and went to the coffee shop without my newspaper, but that cold dice table stuck in my mind all day. The day went by uneventfully: a little golf, some business meetings, a dip in the pool. You know the routine. By evening, I was ready to hit the casino for some serious craps shooting.

I have a habit of thoroughly checking out the tables before I play, and sometimes I feel as if I've walked a mile before I sense an opportunity. The only table that looked good, strangely enough, was the same table that had been so frightfully cold that same morning. The casino was jammed, all the tables were jumping, but only one table was winning—that one. No way would I play it! So I drifted over to the blackjack tables and eventually found a nice spot where the dealer sure knew how to bust. Within a few minutes I was up about $400, winning two out of three hands. During my play, I couldn't help but hear the occasional cheers coming from the dice table, that same table. I tried to tune it out, play my cards, and concentrate on my count. I was winning: Why risk a change when you're winning?

Well, I'll tell you why. When something inside of you is screaming to get over there, you move. I moved. I scooped up my chips and hurried to the table while there was still a spot open. The shooter was rolling for 10, so I threw out a $25 come bet. I noticed that he had a very large pass line bet and all the numbers covered. The other players were big shooters too, with chips all over the table. My come bet went to the 9, so I tossed double odds (the best you could find at the time) to the dealer, and before he could place it on top of my come bet, the shooter threw another 9! I made another come bet for $50, tossed out the odds when the shooter threw a 5, and covered the 6 and 8 with place bets for $60 each. I can't explain the feeling that came over me: It was like some fairy had touched me with her magic wand. I felt extremely relaxed, but the action at the table seemed to zip by in fast-forward. Was I having a premonition? No, it was more than that. I would have bet the proverbial farm if I had owned one. I knew, positively, that this guy was going to make his 10!

You know my rule about starting out with large bets—you don't do it! And I don't do it. But this was different: It was more than a feeling I had, more than my intuitive senses working overtime. It was as if a pair of 5's were bouncing around in my head. I couldn't get them out of my head if I had wanted to. And I'm not sure that I did.

I bought the 10 for $300 (my winnings from the blackjack table). Remember, I got to the table late and didn't have a line bet, so that was the right way to bet it. I had just dumped nearly all of my bankroll for the evening on the table. I didn't realize it at the time, but even if I had, it wouldn't have made any difference. If I had had more money, I would have bet that too. I threw out all I had left—a green chip—for the hard 10 just seconds before the table jumped two feet! And what a commotion! The shooter made his 10! But I wasn't excited, can you believe it? If you knew you were going to win through some rigged bet, would you be excited if you won? Hardly. And that's exactly the way I felt.

When the dealer gave me seven more green chips that I didn't expect, I told him that they weren't mine. He said, "They're yours, sir. It's your hardway. He made the point with two 5's." As it turned out, I had just caught the tail end of a darn good shoot. But I left the table with over $5,000 in winnings, darn good for those years, and awfully darn good for a table that couldn't put two passes together 15 hours earlier.

What was different? It wasn't the dice, although they probably were different. But dice are dice. They are all manufactured to within tolerances of one ten-thousandth of an inch. The math geeks who study this game inside and out will tell you that the chances of that guy making his 10 that evening were exactly the same as if he had been shooting that morning, a time when I wouldn't play. And my answer to them is exactly that: The difference is time. You'll never find "time" as part of any gambling equation. You won't find the gurus of the games talking about hot tables or cold tables either, because in the most technical sense, there really is no such thing. As long as the decisions are purely random events, the guys with the pocket protectors are absolutely right—but they make lousy craps shooters!

Here's the classic battle of logic versus feelings. We know there's no sinister control over dice at a cold table to keep them cold and take all of our money. We know there's no sound reason for playing boldly at a hot table just because some guy has put together a few passes. This issue nags at all players. You know the logic irrefutably, but you can't set aside your feelings. Nor should you.

THE BATTLE OF THE SEXES

I'll never forget the response I got when I once told an audience of gamblers that I thought women were better players overall than men. I heard boos from the guys and a nice round of applause from the ladies. Not a politically smart statement to make, but I wasn't looking for votes; I was looking for traits. It was my humble opinion then and it is my humble opinion today that the best player traits belong to women. Here's my scorecard:

KNOWLEDGE

As a book publisher, I'm well aware of bookseller surveys showing that women account for nearly 80 percent of book purchases. "Yeah, right," say the guys, "but they're buying 'em for us to read." I don't think so. "Yeah, right," say the guys again, "but most of the stuff they buy are romance novels." Wrong again. Take out the paperbacks with those erotic covers and you still have over two-thirds of the buying power. Women are readers. When they find something new in their life—a new interest, maybe even a new husband—they'll go out and get a book about it. Knowledge is power.

PATIENCE

Hands down, women are more patient than men. Guys are always in a hurry to play and too often, it leads to marathon sessions. Women know how to take breaks, relax, and wait for an opportunity.

CAUTION

I rarely see women putting themselves at great initial risk in a casino. The skepticism installed in the fairer sex is a worthy attribute. It even has a name: It's called "a woman's intuition." Women tend to look deeper into what's behind a face or a facade. And, boy, what a facade the casino can put up, right? Absolutely. A confident gambler looks at a casino and its games somewhat cynically.

SHOPPING

Really now, are you going to tell me that men are better shoppers than women? I don't think so either. Shopping for casino games is a huge part of the game plan. Don't just take what casino A is offering. Look at Casino B, and Casino C, and Casino D. Blackjack rules and video poker pay tables are the prime examples. But all games, at least to some extent, vary widely among casinos.

AGGRESSIVENESS

The only important gambling attribute less remarkable among women is aggressiveness. Sure, guys are more aggressive, but are they more aggressive at the right time or just all the time? Regardless, the guys win this round of our little stereotype game. And that's all it is. Top sociologists say that these stereotypes—good or bad—are thinning out as time marches along. I couldn't agree more. I'm reminded of the lady poker player who thinned *me* out last year in an Atlantic City poker tournament. She got everything but the gold in my teeth!

FIVE POWERFUL CONCEPTS

1. Knowledge can put you in control.
2. I can think of no place where patience is more of a virtue than in a casino.
3. A casino is no place to be in a trusting mood.
4. A good shopper finds the best bargains. A poor shopper pays too much.
5. A good gambler is aggressive only at the right times.

DEJA VU

In the earlier chapters on what I called "basic training," I preached the importance of keeping your play in the short term. I said that you can't play a negative-expectation game and hope to beat the casinos over the long term, but you could beat them over the weekend. Remember? Well, what about *two* weekends? Here's a story that should warm every gambler's heart.

A big, off-strip casino in Las Vegas had the surprise of its life one weekend when one of its best customers—a "whale," as casinos like to call them—had one heck of a time at the tables. Here was a player who always—that's *always*—left a big chunk of money behind when he flew home. He'd bet all the numbers at the dice tables—that was his usual plan—and hope for a hot shoot, a shoot that rarely came.

But it came this time, and he was the one who brought it to life. He had the dice; in fact, he had the dice for nearly an hour! He amassed a cool fortune that stunned the hotel—he won a near-record $883,000! But there's more good news. For the player, that is—he went home with it, all of it! He won it on the day he was leaving town.

Well, the casino bosses couldn't wait to get this "loser" back in the hotel. They offered him everything, even offered to fly out and pick him up at his home in Oklahoma in the hotel's private jet. It took some coaxing, but exactly two months to the day after this shooter of all shooters hit the hotel so hard, here he was back again. That's right. He returned to the scene of the crime. But not just to the hotel, but to the same table! The same crew!

We can all write the end to this story, am I right? Or would you prefer to write the ending in typical storybook fashion? Well, this story isn't fiction. It isn't Hollywood. I'll have to tell you how it ended, how it *really* ended. The big guy wrote out his big marker and waited for the dice to get to him. It didn't take long before he proceeded to continue from where he had left off. He had just taken a break, that's all, a two-month break.

Numbers and numbers and more numbers—and more money to take home. He hit 'em again, this time for $195,000. You can do the math yourself: He won well over a million dollars!

So is he coming back? Apparently not. The casino bosses haven't seen his face since. The last time they got on the phone and tried to get him back, he kept the conversation short. He said only two words, two words that might suggest that our "loser" will never be a loser again: "I'm happy."

THE CARDOZA CRAPS MASTER

Exclusive Offer! - Not Available Anywhere Else)

Three Big Strategies!

Here It is! **At last**, the **secrets** of the **Grande-Gold Power Sweep, Molliere's Monte Carlo Turnaround** and the **Montarde-D'Girard Double Reverse** - three big strategies - are made available and presented for the **first time anywhere!** These powerful strategies are designed for the serious craps player, one wishing to bring the best odds and strategies to hot tables, cold tables and choppy tables.

I. THE GRANDE-GOLD POWER SWEEP (HOT TABLE STRATEGY)

This **dynamic strategy** takes maximum advantage of hot tables and shows you how to amass small **fortunes quickly** when numbers are being thrown fast and furious. The Grande-Gold stresses aggressive betting on wagers the house has no edge on! This previously unreleased strategy will make you a powerhouse at a hot table.

2. MOLLIERE'S MONTE CARLO TURNAROUND (COLD TABLE STRATEGY)

For the player who likes betting against the dice, Molliere's Monte Carlo Turnaround shows how to turn a cold table into hot cash. Favored by an exclusive circle of professionals who will play nothing else, the uniqueness of this strongman strategy is that the vast majority of bets **give absolutely nothing away to the casino!**

3.MONTARDE-D'GIRARD DOUBLE REVERSE (CHOPPY TABLE STRATEGY)

This **new** strategy is the **latest development** and the **most exciting strategy** to be designed in recent years. **Learn how** to play the optimum strategies against the tables when the dice run hot and cold (a choppy table) with no apparent reason. **The Montarde-d'Girard Double Reverse** shows how you can **generate big profits** while less knowledgeable players are ground out by choppy dice. And, of course, the majority of our bets give nothing away to the casino!

BONUS!!! Order now, and you'll receive **The Craps Master-Professional Money Management Formula** ($15 value) **absolutely free!** Necessary for serious players and **used by the pros,** the Craps Master Formula features the unique **stop-loss ladder.**

The Above Offer is Not Available Anywhere Else. You Must Order Here.

To order send $75 $50 (plus postage and handling) by check or money order to:
Cardoza Publishing, P.O. Box 98115, Las Vegas, NV 89193

142